A Development Experience Based on Skills

SUCCESS IS HUMAN

Harness the Power of Human Skills and Maximize Potential

by Renata Sguario and Erica Yvonnet

Black Rose Writing | Texas

©2023 by Renata Sguario and Erica Yvonnet
All rights reserved. No part of this book may be reproduced, stored in a retrieval system or transmitted in any form or by any means without the prior written permission of the publishers, except by a reviewer who may quote brief passages in a review to be printed in a newspaper, magazine or journal.

The author grants the final approval for this literary material.

First printing

This is a work of fiction. Names, characters, businesses, places, events, and incidents are either the products of the author's imagination or used in a fictitious manner. Any resemblance to actual persons, living or dead, or actual events is purely coincidental.

ISBN: 978-1-68513-191-3
PUBLISHED BY BLACK ROSE WRITING
www.blackrosewriting.com

Printed in the United States of America
Suggested Retail Price (SRP) $21.95

Success is Human is printed in Garamond Premier

*As a planet-friendly publisher, Black Rose Writing does its best to eliminate unnecessary waste to reduce paper usage and energy costs, while never compromising the reading experience. As a result, the final word count vs. page count may not meet common expectations.

To all the people who have instilled in us a love for learning and have demonstrated a passionate approach for helping others, this book is for you.

ACKNOWLEDGMENTS

All our gratitude, first and foremost, to the universe for providing us with abundant opportunities that have allowed us to experience love, growth, and success.

Thank you to our families, extended families, and friends who have always been so incredibly supportive of our book and of us. We are so appreciative of having such a wonderful network in our lives.

We couldn't have done this without Jay Schell, who, even on vacation and into the late hours of the night, read every word that we wrote.

Our sincere appreciation goes to our fellow author and friend Kristin A. Sherry for her deep expertise and for helping us grow as authors. We could not have done this without her kindness.

A huge thank you goes to our beta readers and our development editor (MEB) who took the time and care to give us valuable feedback on the book.

We'd also like to thank team Maxme as well as our many LinkedIn connections and followers who have all been endlessly supportive of our content contributions.

SUCCESS IS
HUMAN

FOREWORD BY KRISTIN A. SHERRY

Your leadership journey will be unique. It might be a slow and steady process, or you might be called upon to lead with little preparation.

Prior to founding YouMap LLC and being an author, I was given the opportunity to lead a team of smart, creative, hardworking people as a Learning & Development leader within a Fortune 20 company.

Here's the thing -- I had no formal experience in L&D when I applied for the job. At the time, I was an Operations Manager. Yet, there was a theme in my career. I had never led an Operations team, nor worked in Data Analytics, or developed software, when I convinced people to hire me in these fields.

Some people are lucky enough to have leaders in their lives who can instill within them the wisdom of what it takes to be successful in this type of scenario.

What I had was a mother who made me keenly aware of my strengths early in life. She created a monster by telling me I could do "big things" with my strengths. This was no surprise since my mother is an Executive Coach. Her philosophy was that coaching was more effective than "parenting." Through this coaching I learned key lessons.

First, as Socrates phrased it, "Know thyself." Self-understanding was the first stepping stone to success.

Secondly, I learned to be a giver. My mother practices superhero-level generosity. Yet, while she is a giver, she isn't a doormat. I've seen her patiently and skillfully hand people their asses, and they thanked her.

I used to say my mother was some kind of witch the way she managed people who behaved like jackasses. This is the third lesson she taught - how to communicate skillfully - especially when the recipient was resistant.

A fourth lesson I learned was to advocate for myself and others. Mom told me again and again, "The squeaky wheel gets the oil." Sometimes the squeaking was for me, oftentimes for others.

Lastly, I watched and learned as my mother skillfully solved problems that came our family's way. Her resourcefulness and creativity was a thing to behold.

This book takes a deep dive into these lessons. It would have come in handy when I started the Learning & Development job I first told you about.

It's easy to start your leadership journey full of hope and optimism. Before long, you begin to learn of discontentment on the team. Though your team could experience the veneer of being self-aware, collaborative, and unified, something will be off beneath the surface.

As time goes on, people will confide in you about their struggles and the associated stress. Interestingly, though, the reality will not match the image presented. You might even feel like you're doing well despite the stress your colleagues are experiencing.

I remember working 45 hours per week, while they clocked upwards of seventy, due to never-ending projects they were volun-told to take on.

As I read through *Success is Human*, a clear understanding of how others can thrive and experience success when similar challenges arise began to take shape in my mind.

I'm glad (and my mother would be glad too) that you've picked up this book. Return to the wisdom it contains. Here's to your success!

–Kristin A. Sherry, YouMap Profile Creator & bestselling author of *YouMap* and *Ready, Set, Coach! Build a Thriving Coaching Business Fast*
Charlotte, NC
September 2022

TABLE OF CONTENTS

WHO THIS BOOK IS FOR
INTRODUCTION/FRAMEWORK

HONESTY — 1
- Your Strengths are Your Unique Superpowers — 2
- Develop Your Strengths and Put Them to Work — 17
- Do Not Completely Ignore Your Weaknesses — 19
- What to do About Those Pesky Weaknesses — 21
- Use Your Strengths and Get into a Flow — 25
- Practice Flow Through Reflection — 29
- Using Strengths to Accomplish Undesirable Tasks — 32
- Place Your Wager on Job Crafting — 35
- Why Self-Aware People need Honesty — 40

UNITY — 43
- Collaboration and Teamwork is the New Black — 45
- Moving from Me to We — 47
- Great Teams Require Effort — 50
- Teams are Multi-Dimensional — 53
- Unity Can still Exist between Different People — 62
- Without Conflict it is Difficult to have True Unity — 70
- How to Manage and Resolve Conflict — 73

MAXIMIZE — 79
- Getting to Know Your Barriers — 81
- The Four Communication Types — 85
- Planning and Crafting Your Message — 88
- Effective Storytelling is Always in Fashion — 94
- Be an Excited Word Nerd — 98
- Find Great Feedback Nerds — 101
- Adapt What You Say — 104
- The Secret Non-Verbal Ingredients — 108
- The Flavors of Visual Communication — 112
- Using Questions Effectively — 116
- Be an Active Listener — 123
- Don't Let Your Worries Consume You — 126
- Response Techniques for Questions — 129
- You can Make a Positive Impact — 132

ADVOCATE — 138

- Recognize Mindfulness and Balance — 140
- Balance is a Quest — 146
- Resilience is Your Lifeboat — 153
- Plant and Grow a Mindset — 166
- Buy Into the K & G Fluff Stories — 176
- Observation makes Actions more Effective — 182
- Set Goals with a Focused Intention — 187
- Commit to Your Goals — 194
- Distractions and Recovery from Setbacks — 201

NAVIGATE — 213

- Let Curiosity Fuel You — 214
- Drive Your Creativity — 217
- Steer Towards Innovation — 221
- Adapt the Disruptive Fog — 225
- Push Your Environment to the Metal — 229
- Shift Your Thinking — 232
- Challenges are Not Roadblock if You're Agile — 239
- Embrace Forks in the Road — 245
- Brake for Company Structure — 248
- Destination Greatness — 252

FINAL THOUGHTS — 253

- Learn More About Maxme
- Speaking Inquiries
- Certifications
- Media
- QR Code, Tools, and Resources
- Works Cited and Notes

ABOUT THE AUTHORS

WHO THIS BOOK IS FOR

This guide exists to equip people with the skills they need to thrive in work and in life. It is for anyone who is interested in maximizing their potential.

INTRODUCTION

We are two women. One of us forged a career path in the world of business and the other in the world of education. Although more than 10,000 miles exist between us, we came together on this project because we wanted to change the way people felt about work.

In both of our industries, we recognized a need for a shift in thinking. Too many people are learning only so they can pass instead of learning the skills they need for life. We wondered: Can a framework be designed for a group of people so that they can collectively obtain success?

What we discovered was that people commonly shared a passion for success but were convinced that their work efforts would not bring them any closer to achievement. They also were disengaged and lacked the desire to channel a great deal of efforts toward activities that would help them succeed. They believed that success remained beyond the reach of many.

This was alarming to us, since we knew that learning could have a greater impact if the person had a vision of where that learning could take them. As we explored a different approach, it became apparent that what people needed was reassurance that the path to becoming successful in work and in life is not as narrow as it seems.

Imagine living in the kind of world that embraces the benefits of practicing self-awareness, communicating with impact, and working together in a cooperative way. Or the kind of world that is filled with professionals who incorporate mindfulness, creativity, and ownership of their behaviors into their daily routines.

It is only when people learn and practice all these human skills that we, as a collective population, can thrive in the workplace and in our lives. And thus, this collaboration was built with a foundation of learning human skills as the outcome.

OUR APPROACH IS THE
Success is Human Framework

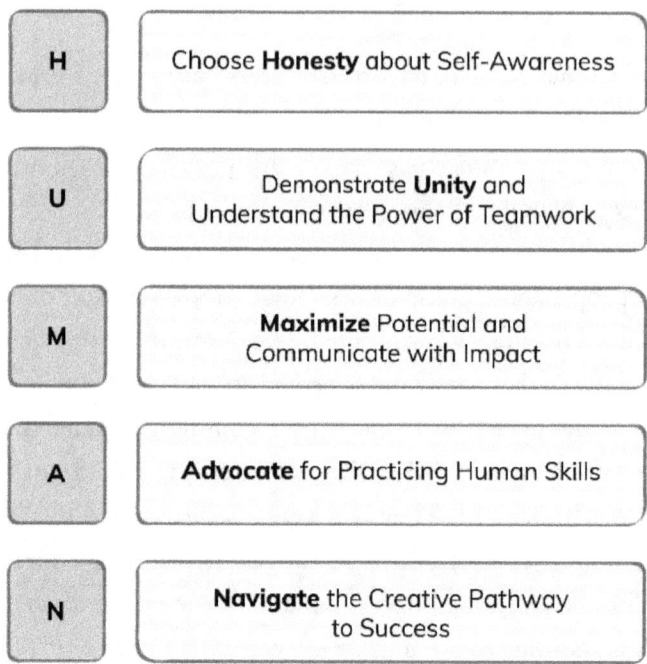

Throughout this book, we will take a deep dive into each of these five pillars. Let's get started.

Part One
"H"
Choose <u>Honesty</u> about Self-Awareness

"Honesty is the first chapter in the book of wisdom."
-Thomas Jefferson[i]

HONESTY

From the time we are small, we are taught to be honest. When little Timmy is caught in a lie, his parents usually sit him down and talk with him about the need to be honest. Sometimes they tell him bedtime stories about little boys just like him who get in trouble for not being honest. As a result, Timmy learns that telling lies is not something good little boys do.

For most people, this trait is encouraged and becomes ingrained in us as we grow. But some people don't tackle the issue of being honest with themselves and practicing *self-awareness* as readily.

What's worse, they end up being adults who are consumed in debt, are unable to build trustworthy relationships, work in a job they loathe going to, and who are generally unhappy due to their inability to define what genuine success looks like for them. This is because people haven't been taught that being honest with yourself means you are willing to listen, empathize, understand, and then act.

As a result, society's intentions to prepare people for a complex world, while nice, fall short of what is truly needed. "Learning to pass" rather than "Learning for life" tends to be the mainstream approach and we fail to nurture what will ultimately set ourselves up for a life well lived in these most complex of times. We do not apologize when we say that we can be better as a society if we practice honesty and self-awareness with ourselves.

Your Unique Strengths are Your Superpowers

Are all people really being honest about recognizing what they can and cannot do? This is not a trick question, but rather an unveiling of truths that we need to be aware of so we can collectively improve.

We need to know who we are, where we are headed, and why. To achieve this, we must stop pretending that we have exhausted all our attempts to close an achievement gap by doing more of the same and expecting something better or different. It also means that we have to successfully stop coveting the strengths of others.

When we don't practice self-awareness, we don't discover our potential, develop meaningful relationships, or learn the required skills to solve problems with people. This is in part the fault of traditional education systems, since they are all about measurement. They measure the points that people receive on exams, they measure what objectives are met in a fiscal year, and they analyze stale data more than they encourage potential.

Having potential is about revealing your superpowers to the world! You might think it strange that we mention superpowers when this book is supposed to be about how to become a successful human, but you read that correctly, SUPERPOWERS. Not the kind that gives you laser vision or invisibility, but the kind that makes you feel empowered and that you are living a life that is filled with success!

Everyone, including you, deserves to learn, discover, and harness their abilities. And once you do, you can increase your positive impact on the world. The good news is your strengths are your superpowers, and they are already part of you. Which means they are what you are good at without even needing to try. They are unique, can be tapped repeatedly, and can be developed. They are the manifestation of your potential, your character, and your traits.

It seems odd to think that so many people are walking around on the track of life and not seeing these natural shortcuts. If it is your goal to see these shortcuts, you need to be self-aware, and this can be done by investing more time focusing on your inherent qualities.

You might be wondering about your weakness because it's common to think that if you want to be a successful person, you should focus on those. This simply is not the truth. When it comes to spending your precious time, focusing on your strengths yields a greater reward. With this knowledge, you can turbo charge your results and give yourself a competitive edge.

So, to harness those superpowers, first, you need to be honest about how you perform. If you work better in a quiet and private space, for example, you should do that as often as possible.

The next way to be self-aware of your qualities is to be honest about what energizes and satisfies your body. For instance, are you getting enough of what you need to make you feel content? Being able to answer this question is necessary so you can reduce stress and release your happy hormones into our societies.

Lastly, be honest about the significance of your contributions towards your personal growth. After you recognize your own strengths, you can then successfully communicate them to others. We will discuss this in a later section.

The fact is, if someone is already strong at a particular skill, they will always outperform a person who is either mediocre or must work hard to feel successful at that skill. You might not realize it, but you are already a uniquely strong and capable person. Focus on what drives your strengths.[ii]

Regardless of how weak you feel sometimes, remember, no one is good at everything. It's okay. Seriously. You can lean on your strengths, or you can tap into someone else's. What's awesome about them is they can be developed from a combination of factors, and they are easier than you think to discover.

Strengths are your superpowers because your strengths are who you are at your core. They are the personality traits and abilities that you express when you are being your authentic self. While there are several models out there that can help people discover, describe, and understand their strengths. The VIA Character Strengths Survey Method[iii] has won us over.

They have done a great job of identifying personal strengths as parts of your personality that impact how you think, feel, and behave. It's a well-established framework, based on global scientific studies, that identifies 24 character strengths in people.

It should be noted that character strengths are divided by virtues as a holistic classification. As follows, "The framework offers cognitive strengths (under the virtue of wisdom), emotional strengths (courage), social and community strengths (humanity and justice), protective strengths (temperance), and spiritual strengths (transcendence)."[iv]

For each of the 24 character strengths listed, read the descriptions, and think about whether the description is very much like you, like you, neutral, unlike you, or very much unlike you.

Cognitive Strengths:

Creativity
Virtue: Wisdom

Character Description
You like finding new ways of doing things. You're constantly thinking of different ways to make sense of the world, solve problems, and express yourself. At work, and in study, you thrive on challenge and appreciate a flexible environment when you're given the room and the support to think outside the box.

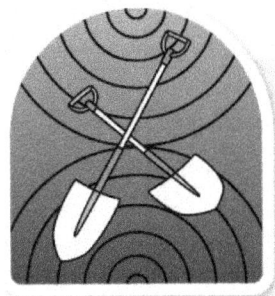

Curiosity
Virtue: Wisdom

Character Description
You like figuring out how things work and why. You enjoy delving into information, engaging in new experiences, and taking action to feed your desires to keep growing. You thrive when tasked with solving a problem or meeting particular goals.

Judgement
Virtue: Wisdom

Character Description
You're a look-before-you leap kind of person. You're able to evaluate information and consider all the possibilities before reaching a conclusion. You're generally open to new ideas and opinions and are able to challenge your personal assumptions.

Love of Learning
Virtue: Wisdom

Character Description
You're an endless provider of interesting facts. You like to increase your knowledge, whether by a reading, taking classes or watching educational TV. You thrive when given the opportunity to use a new skill or further develop your knowledge.

Perspective
Virtue: Wisdom

Character Description
You see the big picture. People often seek you out for your advice that helps them make sense of the world. Often described as wise beyond your years, you thrive when engaged in tasks that draw on your experiences and expertise.

Bravery
Virtue: Courage

Character Description
Never one to shy away from a challenge, you're in your element when confronting and making the best of them. You feel fear, but it's your ability to act inspite of these feelings. This allows you to push for the interests of others.

Emotional Strengths:

Perseverance
Virtue: Courage

Character Description
You get the job done! Setting goals and working hard to reach them, you're willing to tough it out through long hours to complete a project. Your dedication helps to pick others up who might've otherwise fallen short of the target.

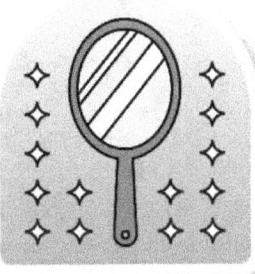

Honesty
Virtue: Courage

Character Description
You tell it like it is. You're authentic, keep your promises and never beat around the bush – people always know where they stand with you. You thrive when doing work that allows you to "walk your talk."

Zest
Virtue: Courage

Character Description
You're full of energy. Completely engaged and enthusiastic about life, you look forward to each day, and this energy is contagious for others. You love to be in the driver's seat of your life, riding the waves of your energy to get the job done.

Love
Virtue: Humanity

Character Description
You're a people person. You care deeply and express compassion for those who matter to you. You put others' needs before your own and take pleasure in being able to build and maintain good relationships.

Social and Community Strengths:

Kindness
Virtue: Humanity

Character Description
You truly enjoy helping others. You normally go out of your way to make other people happy. This gives you great personal satisfaction because you love knowing that your actions have positively impacted someone else's day.

Social Intelligence
Virtue: Humanity

Character Description
You're great at reading people. You notice people's emotions, can size up their intentions, understand what makes them tick and respond accordingly. You find this "people knowledge" useful and beneficial in group situations.

Teamwork
Virtue: Justice

Character Description
You're at your best working with others, rather than alone, and feel a strong sense of loyalty and commitment. You thrive in groups and are often referred to as a team player.

Fairness
Virtue: Justice

Character Description
You keep things just and strive for fairness. You have a strong sense of what you believe to be right and act accordingly. You care deeply about others and want to do the right thing by them.

Leadership
Virtue: Justice

Character Description
You have a knack for motivating others to take action and reach their goals. You enjoy planning group activities, and others turn to you for direction. You often assume responsibility for setting goals, key decisions, challenges, and successes.

Forgiveness
Virtue: Temperance

Character Description
You rarely hold a grudge. For you, feeling good in life is only possible when you let go of hurt feelings and forgive people for their mistakes. You believe in giving others a second chance and learning from any disagreements.

Protective Strengths:

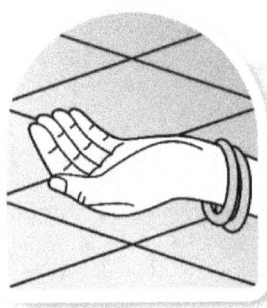

Humility
Virtue: Temperance

Character Description
You'd rather blend into the crowd than stand out. You're able to put others' needs before your own and feel that others play a big part in your success. While you recognize your strengths and successes, you prefer not to publicize them.

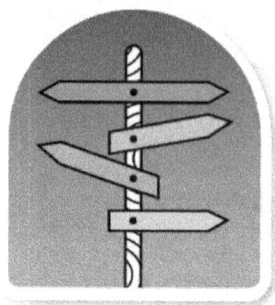

Prudence
Virtue: Temperance

Character Description
You keep things on track. As someone who values a good plan, you are good at regulating your behaviors. You strive when you're able to take a structured path to deliver results.

Self-Regulation
Virtue: Temperance

Character Description
You're the master of managing your urges. You're able to control your impulses, desires, and emotions. You thrive when work and life feel balances, ordered, and progressing towards your goals.

Appreciation of Beauty and Excellence
Virtue: Transcendence

Character Description
You like things that are done well. You really notice the things going on around you as you walk around, read, listen or watch things. A lover of fine things, nature, art, literature, and/or science, you thrive in environments where good work is encouraged, admired & valued.

Spiritual Strengths:

Gratitude
Virtue: Transcendence

Character Description
You're thankful for all the good things in your life. In addition to savoring the positive things in your own life, you appreciate the chance to thank others and to be thanked by them.

Hope
Virtue: Transcendence

Character Description
You're a glass-half-full kind of person. You expect the best for the future and regularly look on the bright side of life, finding positives where others might see only negatives. When things don't go to plan, you believe that tomorrow will be better than today, and that fuels you to stay positive and keep going.

Humor
Virtue: Transcendence

Character Description
You have to make people laugh. You like to focus on the lighter side of life and not take yourself too seriously. You make the ordinary seem livelier and put others at ease in times of stress, often using your humor to encourage and uplift others.

Spirituality
Virtue: Transcendence

Character Description
You have a clear sense of meaning and purpose, and it brings you great comfort. Your beliefs influence everything you do, and as a result, you thrive when you're able to participate in work that feels meaningful, is aligned to your values, and benefits others.

If you're not confident about what your top strengths are, no need to worry. Everyone expresses all 24 traits to different levels. Knowing which you rate highest on can help you reveal your character superpowers.

Don't believe us? Try it. Take the survey. Why? According to the website, "The VIA Survey is the only free, scientific survey of character strengths in the world." It also receives bonus points since it only takes fifteen minutes.

Take the survey by going to this link or scanning the QR code.
https://www.viacharacter.org/account/register

See what we mean? It gave us chills when we first took it too. By the way, resist the urge to feed your negativity bias and don't waste time obsessing over the strengths that you ranked as "unlike me" or "very much unlike me." Instead, force yourself to admire and focus on the strengths that are "very much like me" or "like me."

Consider this: if you had money to invest in a project or a company and you wanted to get a quick return, would you invest your hard-earned cash in something that's already doing well or something that isn't? Be honest!

Put simply, we all know that companies get higher returns on investment when they focus on what they have already accomplished (strengths) and a lower or slower return when they invest in ideas that are unproven or less desirable (weaknesses).

The research on recognizing your potential by focusing on strengths says a lot. Gallup[v], for example, is an analytics and advice company that surveyed a vast group of people across the globe. They discovered that people who use their strengths in everyday activities are three times more likely to report an excellent quality of life and six times more likely to be successful in their careers.

This mindset can also be practiced with young people. In the Gallup study, people were split into two groups: highly talented readers and average readers and identified each group as such. Both groups were given the same speed-reading improvement training over the same period of time. The average readers improved by 66%; they went from reading 90 words per minute to 150 words per minute. Not bad.

What was truly exceptional was the highly talented reading group improved by 828%. Whoa! They went from 350 words per minute to 2,900 words per minute!

Not only did we find this incredible, but it really drives our point home. While average readers improved, the larger gain came to those who were improving a strength they already had. Focusing on improving your unique superpowers will clearly give you the biggest bang for your buck (or time). It is now your turn to have these kinds of results.

Develop Your Strengths and Put Them to Work

It might surprise you, but "Only 1 in 4 people use their strengths every day. That means 3 in 4 people are not performing to the best of their ability daily."[vi]

This is the case because the sad truth is that, particularly when people are young, they spend so much of their time focusing and sometimes obsessing about how exceptional they think other people are. When in reality, they have strengths of their own to focus on. You can be the exception.

You are a unique treasure. Use this information to take advantage of your strengths as your true superpowers! Achieve this by taking an honest look at them so you can learn about other aspects that make up your strengths. Then you can take advantage of them.

What we know about strengths is that they develop over time and result from the investment in our natural talent and character. Everyone is born with different natural talents, but only when people invest in their talents and develop them through lots of practice do they become strengths that can eventually turn into skills. These skills make us strong, they make us stand out, and they differentiate us from the rest of the pack.

A great example of using and developing strengths is Michael Jordan. No doubt Michael Jordan had talent in basketball, but he also had the character qualities needed to become successful and used them to anchor his every move. Fiercely tenacious, determined, and persistent, he invested many years into developing his strengths. As a result, he became arguably the best player of his generation. It is unlikely that the Chicago Bulls would have won six NBA championship titles in eight years without his commitment to using his strengths.

If you're wondering how to unleash your inner Michael Jordan, now is the time to tell you it all starts with your willingness to let go of your negative views of yourself. Start digging for the gold within you. This might seem easier said than done, but if you've completed your character strengths survey, you've already done some solid gold-detection work.

Those character strengths are your superpowers ready to charge your performance. They are your character kryptonite that can impede your success if they are not managed well. The most powerful way you can develop your strengths and put them to work is the ability to craft your own personal strengths statement. It's what people use for applying to jobs, when they are in interviews, when they are having performance conversations, or when they are pitching themselves for a promotion.

This is the story you will tell to reveal your strengths to other people. Since this will provide others the first impression of you, it should be a quick and convincing share about who you are and what you can contribute to a new team.

Being able to confidently speak about yourself is key here, especially if you are trying to get a promotion or searching for a job. Your statement is literally a phrase that aims to convince someone to choose you over others. Remember that personal strength statements should be personal, show development, and be written in alignment with your unique strengths.

For example, if your strength is honesty, you might say, *"I have been successful when using my strength of honesty because people know I am authentic and always keep my word, which helps me build trust and strong working relationships. An example of that is when I was recently asked to help organize my school reunion. There were many things that needed to be done and I happily committed to taking on some important tasks and getting them done as promised. I got a special mention on the night, which felt great."*

If your strength is teamwork, you might say, *"Teamwork is a strength of mine, and I really enjoy my work when I get the opportunity to team up with others to support and inspire each other to achieve great things together. An example of this is my last team project, where I started every team meeting with a quick check-in with each team member on their 'project energy level.' This allowed me to actively identify opportunities to help lift anyone who might need a boost. It always feels great to give energy to others, especially in a team environment."*

Do Not Completely Ignore Your Weaknesses

Sometimes the struggle is real. This might be a side effect of your weaknesses. We know we mentioned how you should not focus on your weaknesses earlier. That's true. Just a clarification here. Your focus should be all on your strengths, but you should definitely be a self-aware person when it comes to your weaknesses.

We believe as Brené Brown did when she said, "At the end of the day, at the end of the week, at the end of my life, I want to be able to say that I contributed more than I criticized."[vii]

Admit it. As a society, we criticize people by labeling them as weak. The word *weakness* itself has such a negative connotation, doesn't it? But weakness is not a bad word, it's simply a lack of strength in something. Nobody, and we mean it, NOBODY is good at everything. That's just a fact. Regardless of how many times you try certain things, you will struggle.

Think about activities you perform that leave you feeling like you have consumed lots of energy and in the end you feel deflated, bored, and even frustrated. You are not alone in spending a lot of precious time and energy feeling inadequate and getting mediocre results. Most people, according to David Pennington[viii], "Spend 80% of their time working in weaknesses and 20% of their time working in strengths."

Everyone has weaknesses. Sometimes we suck at doing something and sometimes we are great at it. When things seem perfect, we have to remember that they are probably staged, fake, or even impossible. The secret sauce of success is to embrace your imperfections and figure out how to amplify the good bits of you to work with the not-so-good bits.

Work with, not against, your weaknesses because they will not change much over time. Instead, they need to be understood, so you stop being defined by them. If not, they will inevitably get in the way or derail something that is very important to you, like achieving your goals.

Honesty, if you are looking for a plan to help turn your weaknesses into strengths, you will not find it in this book. Our researched and tested philosophy is to work with and manage your weaknesses while maximizing your strengths. In our experience, this is the road to high performance and personal success.

Think about your weaknesses objectively. It's your ability to identify them and honestly reflect on them that will give you the valuable information you need. A good way to gain perspective is to ask for feedback from other people. But before you do, ask yourself, "Am I open to feedback when I receive it?"

Warning! Feedback can be difficult and scary to ask for and receive. When you hear negative stuff about yourself, it can be a tough pill to swallow. But feedback can also be very insightful if it comes from someone you trust.

This process can be especially useful in helping you identify potential blind spots, the things that other people notice about you that you were previously unaware of. For instance, you might be lacking your character strengths awareness or perhaps you are overusing a strength.

There are a couple of questions you can ask yourself through this process, and you might find that the feedback process can be enjoyable. Remember to consider if the feedback is coming from someone you trust and if that person knows you well.

Consider asking yourself questions such as: Does this person have my back, and are they giving me feedback to help me? Have I heard this before? Is this really who I am or am I just having a bad day? Is there any truth to what I am hearing?

When answering these questions, be honest about how open you are to feedback or if you are just listening from a defensive perspective, which happens. Honesty is important, as it can bring you awareness of both your strengths, weaknesses, and things that you may not have known about yourself before.

What to do About Those Pesky Weaknesses

At this point you might be saying, "Okay, so I'm more aware of my weaknesses than ever before, GREAT! Now what?" No need to worry. Here are four tips to help you deal with your weaknesses, or what we like to call lesser strengths. Since you don't want your lesser strengths to be your character kryptonite and get in the way of your success, these tips will help you manage them.

Pro Tip #1: Don't waste time trying to make them into strengths. This can take months and months of daily disciplined practice to even have a slight chance of making one of your lesser strengths into a strength to write home about. That's a whole lot of energy-draining effort for a "maybe this will become a strength" opportunity.

For example, if teamwork isn't your strong suit and self-regulation isn't your forte, these are not things that are going to magically become superpowers, regardless of the amount of time you put into them. So, embrace them as lesser strengths.

Pro Tip #2: Do yourself a favor and check if your weakness is an overused strength. Overusing your strength to the point where it becomes a weakness might sound strange. The best way to explain this is with an example:

Let's say we know this girl named Sara. She's outgoing, bubbly, and she finds it easy to connect with people. Did I mention she inspires people to act? That too. This is because Sara's top strength is zest! So basically, she can fill a room and people with a lot of energy.

Lately however, Sara noticed that people have been avoiding her calls, and when she is in a room, she is seeing more and more eye rolls. At first, she is really surprised about this. Then she starts to feel down on herself. So, what does she do? She decides to ask one of her friends for some honest feedback. What she discovers is that her friends think she doesn't always read the room and sometimes she just needs to be a little more relaxed.

Sara reflects on this feedback and realizes she has been overusing her strength of zest. So, she makes a choice to dial down her strength in certain social situations. After a while, things go back into balance, and Sara has gained a new awareness that she didn't have before. She now can manage the overuse of this strength in the future.

Pro Tip #3: Dial up a strength to work with a weakness. This might seem like a bizarre recommendation, but keep reading for an example that will help shed light on how to do this. Basically, there are two ways you can use a strength to balance out or get around a weakness. Option A - Dial up one of your own strengths, or Option B - Balance out your weakness by finding someone else with the strength you need.

Before we discuss the options, let's meet Ben, who has found himself in a situation where he must dial up one of his top strengths to counter his weakness in a big way. He is struggling with prudence, which means he isn't great at keeping things on track.

You see, the problem here is that Ben isn't fazed when details are not attended to, and it's starting to affect his results, which are coming later than he had hoped. Ben realizes that this is having an impact on him because now he is working on a team with four other people, and they are trying to complete a group task.

The group all wants to smash this task and achieve significant results, so they have all agreed that they need to work hard to stay on track. Ben quickly falls behind because of his lack of prudence, and the rest of the group gets angry and annoyed at him.

In general, Ben seems relaxed about the situation, but he doesn't like the way the group is acting toward him, and he doesn't understand why they are upset. So, what can Ben do? He can make a plan to dial up one of his own top strengths and make more of an effort to get around a weakness. Ben is really wondering what's going on. He doesn't mean to annoy people and doesn't like how this feels, so he thinks about what he can do.

He decides to use one of his top strengths of social intelligence (great at reading people) and observes his group's behavior towards him and asks them a couple of good questions. As a result, he realizes he wasn't being honest with himself about his weakness. Now he knows that the team needs him to step up his work effort and make sure that he is getting the job done as promised.

Ben apologies to his group and promises not to let his team down. This new awareness of what is causing his team's behavior means that Ben can now have an open and honest conversation with the team and get his work back on track. He will also need to dial up his prudence because, even though it won't be easy, Ben knows what the team needs, and he doesn't want to let them down.

However, if Ben knows just attempting to dial up prudence might not work on its own, he can formulate a better plan. Ben realizes he knows someone that has Prudence as their top strength, and that person is his sister.

She is an epic planner and gets stuff done on time, every time. Even though Ben always teased her about this, he now knows this is one of her strengths and she can probably help him with his lesser strength of prudence.

Ben asks his sister to help him pull together a plan to have some accountability and get back on track for his assignment. His sister makes him appropriately grovel but finally agrees to help her brother out. Ben realizes that this might be hard but asks his sister to check on him every couple days to make sure he keeps on track.

Pro Tip #4: Be realistic. Weaknesses or lesser strengths are something that all humans have. The ability to excel at everything is not realistic, but neither is turning something we are not good at into a strength. Be aware of how to prevent them from getting in your way. Knowing your weaknesses strengthens you.

Let's Try Writing
About Your Lesser Strengths

For this exercise:
Remember to consider the four tips. Then answer the question, "What are some ways you can deal with your weaknesses or lesser strengths?"

Write your response here:

Use Your Strengths to Get into a Flow

To be honest, understanding your strengths is not enough. To get their full benefit, you have to learn to power up your work or study by using your strengths every single day. Welcome to the game of maximizing your efforts. It's a path to glory where people find reward in developing their strengths.

One highly effective way to fine-tune or maximize your strengths is by working "in a state of flow."

Meet flow, your powerful companion in positive psychology that was developed by psychologist Mihaly Csikszentmihalyi.[ix] Everyone needs more flow in their life. Flow is the state that people enter when they are engrossed in a task that requires their full attention. It's been called many names such as "in the zone" or "in the groove."

Here is the good news in the form of a math problem when it comes to flow: Using your strengths = more likely to enter a state of flow AND using your strengths in the flow = your skills get developed. Eventually, in time, your development will be maximized, and this will continue to supercharge your strengths. Enter winning.

Everyone loves to win, and supercharged strengths make you feel that way. You will feel more alive, energized, and alert. Ever wonder how some people seem to tap into hidden reserves of energy and enthusiasm? It's your friend flow.

With flow, things just work. You're more creative, better at problem-solving, and you can make better decisions. Doubts fall away and self-confidence soars. In fact, dare we say you'll feel a greater sense of freedom because you will know you can achieve what you need to do?

Imagine feeling like you have laser focus. Picture brushing aside all distractions or not even noticing them to begin with. Envision time flying because you are so engrossed in what you are doing that you have no idea you have been in a state of flow for so long.

Flow is undeniably beneficial. It brings learning, improvement, growth, and advancement into your life. It creates a level of satisfaction and pride in your achievements like nothing else can. If you want to stop feeling helpless or overwhelmed and you want to have better clarity on who you are at your best, traveling with flow is the way.

So, pack flow as the gift that keeps on giving into your success suitcase and recognize that the more often you get into a state of flow, the easier it becomes to enter it again and again. This can amplify your skills even more.

How to tap into that magical flow feeling, you ask? You enter a state of flow when you perform tasks that challenge you to an appropriate extent for your skill level. Here's the thing, you need to find the sweet spot of what appropriate is.

If the task is too challenging or not challenging enough for your skill level, you may fall into an undesired and unhelpful state of mind. Remember boredom? It gets in the way of successfully completing your tasks.

Instead, you must be ready to break down tasks that are too challenging into smaller "chunks" or "jazz-up" tasks that are too easy and not challenging enough to keep you psyched about them. It should also be noted that getting and staying in the flow cannot happen if you are watching the clock or rushing through your task so you can just get back to what's most important to you.

If you are feeling distracted, stop and take time to address what is distracting you and then get back to it. If you want to succeed, make sure that your goals are clear and allow these deeper levels of concentration into your life.

You can achieve flow by using the right strength at the right time. Basically, you need to create more flow moments by intentionally applying your strengths. If you're clear on what you want to achieve and why, it will be easier to identify which strength you need to dial up or down to get there.

The first flow-focused step you will need to take is developing a clear path. This is related to the task you will perform, what you want to achieve, and by when. Try to think about any challenges or anticipate mistakes that the task may present so that you can be ready when it happens.

As an example, let's say you need to write an essay on a topic that you don't really understand well. You should not just sit there playing with your phone and hope the essay will magically write itself. It won't. Your first step should probably be to designate a place to get started. You can use this as an entry point on the path ahead. You might decide to do some research. Once you have your start defined or underway, here are some things to keep in mind:

Pro Tip #1: Display your strengths. Have a list of your top strengths in a visible space on your desk or computer as a reminder of which strengths you should use most often. Save them on your phone or put them in a daily reminder. Heck, make a t-shirt if you think it will help. The point is that they need to be the first thing you see and read when you wake up.

Pro Tip #2: Read your inner mood. Be aware of your emotions when performing tasks. If you are feeling engaged, calm, aligned, and grounded, that's a good sign you're in the flow. The opposite is also true. If you're feeling bored, disinterested, anxious, over-excited, or exhausted, then you are not in the flow. Be patient with yourself and take a moment to work through what might be stopping you. Take a breath. Try and relax. Think.

Pro Tip #3: Find your peak times. Most people have an ideal time of day in which to get into the flow, and you should become familiar with what time of day you perform at your best. It's important to know your own chronotype or body clock. Everyone experiences fluctuations of energy throughout the day, but ask yourself this question: "Are you a lark, owl, or hummingbird? or most commonly referred to as a morning or night person?" Understanding this will help you work out when you are going to be the most productive.

Pro Tip #4: Take small steps and practice a lot. Face this truth. You need to find small ways to integrate your strengths more into your day-to-day tasks. Keep pushing yourself each day. This will be hard, but not feeling successful is also hard. Choose your hard.

Practice Flow Through Reflection

Learning to use your strengths is a process. Some days will produce better results than others. The key is to remind yourself that trying your best and being the best version of yourself has something in common. Reflection.

Reflection should happen during and after an attempt to get into the flow. It is important and is the reason successful people know what gives them energy versus what drains them. It is also the reason why, if they are not using all their strengths, they know how to change their approach.

You can practice your flow by frequently reflecting on your performance. This involves taking time to evaluate what went well and what didn't. It also involves the willingness to acknowledge your feelings, make corrections, and try again.

Ideally, flow should feel like this:

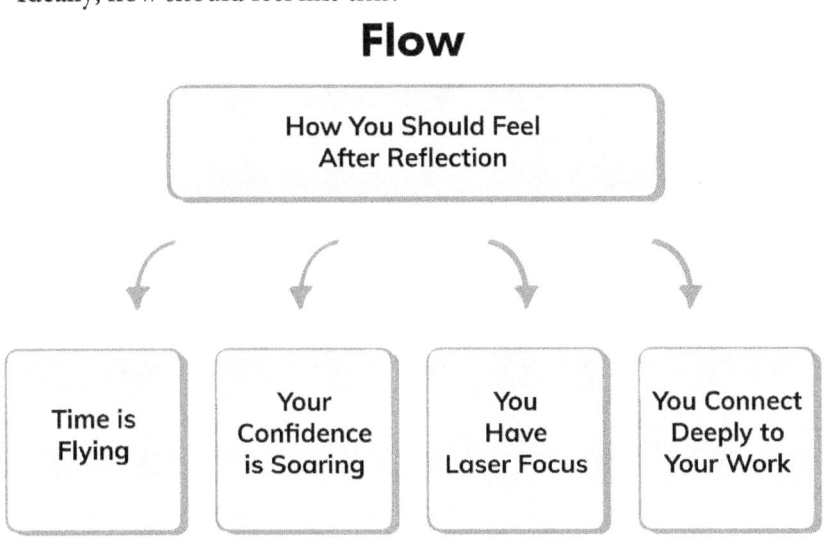

In addition to your feelings, during your flow reflection, you should also reflect on your strengths. Use too little of a strength and you might feel like you are not reaching a state of flow. While overusing a strength can make you feel burnt out and incapable of obtaining flow.

Take, for instance, our friend, let's call her Amelia. She feels down on herself because she finds confrontation scary. She has top strengths of honesty and fairness and a lesser strength of bravery.

It's important to Amelia to be honest, and she likes to feel like people are being honest back. She also enjoys seeing people being treated fairly. When that is not the case, Amelia gets frustrated and sometimes she even gets angry.

And let's not forget her lesser strengths that can get in the way of her top strengths shining. Unfortunately, for Amelia, bravery is a lesser strength. She doesn't want to come across as a mean person by being too honest on unfair, so she is unlikely to be brave and say something to people when there is a conflict. Reflection can help identify when this is the case too.

Reflection can help when strengths and lesser strengths negatively affect your flow. What's worse, if you don't reflect often, your feelings of frustration will get the better of you and over time, this will really start to impact your well-being and success.

But how do you make corrections? By asking yourself daily questions about your feelings and strengths.

At the end of each day, spend a few minutes and honestly respond to the following questions:

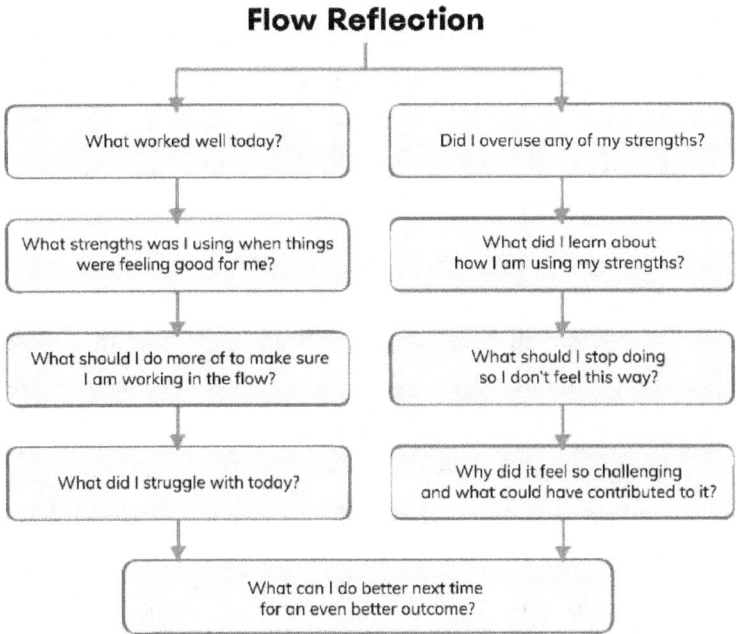

When you reflect on the moments you are in and out of flow, you will feel better about harnessing the power of your strengths. This practice will bring you closer to being your best self.

Your brain will remember this. This process may seem a bit forced until it becomes a habit. Try it. Stick with it. You may surprise yourself.

Using Strengths to Accomplish Undesirable Tasks

A lot of ground has been covered on how to discover, understand, develop, and use your strengths. For most of you, it's suspected that this might be the first time you are looking at yourself through such a clear frame.

However, not everything dovetails neatly with our strengths. In a perfect world, every task we must do would be more fun and enjoyable. But that's not reality. Work is work. And while it's pretty easy to get through the stuff you like to do, getting through the stuff you don't enjoy doing is where you need to dig deep.

Truth be told, we all have things we need to do that are less desirable and require far more motivation. You know they're important activities to complete, but they are tedious, sometimes painful, and always less appealing than what's on Netflix this week. Bet you are thinking about something you must do right now that you really don't want to do, like completing your yearly tax return.

While some might find watching paint dry thrilling, in these dreadful moments, think about how you can use your strengths to make the whole thing less painful. For example, you can try expressing humor or kindness to your accountant, and maybe they will (in gratitude) inform you of tax breaks you had not considered. Bonus points! This will also make someone smile and help you get into the flow.

The secret here is to look through the lens of a top strength in order to lighten the way you feel about a dreaded task. This is illustrated by our new "friend" Victoria.

Victoria hates cooking and is inexperienced in culinary arts, but she promised to cook her family dinner at her new place. However, Victoria's top strength is love, so to help her deal with this challenge, she thinks about how good her family will feel knowing she is cooking a special meal for them. That approach turns a frustrating experience into a pleasant one.

You can improve your attitude towards doing something you don't want to do by having more fun with it. Put some music on, dance like no one is watching you, wear a silly hat, basically do whatever makes you feel happy, and then go back to focusing on your strengths and the task when you feel the difference.

Earl Nightingale said, "A great attitude does much more than turn on the lights in our worlds; it seems to magically connect us to all sorts of serendipitous opportunities that were somehow absent before the change."[x] We agree. Keep going and fill your life with moments of beneficial things!

But what do you do if you've hit a wall? No worries, pause and think about how you can surge in that strength, and this will help you get through it. Take another peer of ours, for example, Levi.

Levi is trying to fight obesity by concentrating on his fitness. So naturally, he begins an exercise routine. This morning he hits a snag. He feels out of energy before reaching his goal for the day. Instead of stopping, Levi uses his strength of curiosity to focus on the leafy trees around him. This makes the task more enjoyable since Levi has always been interested in horticulture and genuinely enjoys thinking about the species of trees around him. This approach takes his mind off the exercise, and as a result, he can finish his task.

In addition to staring at the leaves, Levi also needs to know that there are three questions that are useful when trying to motivate himself to complete a project, task, or goal. Only he can answer them. You can answer them for yourself later, if you'd like.

Questions to Motivate Yourself

WHY	HOW	WHO
is it important to you?	are you going to get your work done using as many strengths as possible?	do you need help from to get this done on time and to a high standard?
....	....	....
....	....	....
....	....	....
....	....	....
....	....	....
....	....	....
....	....	....

Once asked these three questions, he added that fitness was important to him because his obesity might contribute to becoming a diabetic like his father. Preventing this fate is his why. He can use his strength of curiosity as well as his other strengths to get the job done. He has leadership as another strength, for example. Perhaps he can organize a group to participate in a 4k run to make himself even more motivated. If he wants to increase his fitness levels in a reasonable amount of time and to a high standard, he can get his friend Victoria to join him in his training for the event as she regularly exercises.

Obviously, you are not Levi or Victoria, and you have your own challenges and a unique list of what you need to do. Once you can answer these three questions successfully, you will find the much-needed motivation and purpose to get any job done.

Place Your Wager on Job Crafting

Developing and improving our self-awareness is a long journey of many steps. Along the way, one useful tool to help you be successful is job crafting.

Job crafting is about taking proactive steps and actions to redefine what you do. It includes using your strengths to alter the way you perform and making the necessary changes to your responsibilities and relationships.

Taking this approach will help you improve your process of completing the tasks on your to-do list. This will also reshape the types of interactions you have since it optimizes the amount of time you need to complete tasks. As a result, you will feel satisfied about your accomplishments.

According to Professor Amy Wrzesniewski,[xi] job crafting happens in three possible ways. These ways are task crafting, relationship crafting, and/or cognitive crafting.

Task crafting is all about changing up your responsibilities so you can get more meaning out of what you spend your time doing. For example, have you met Gary yet? He needs to create a new method of filing to make his job seem less repetitive. His goal is to do as little filing as possible, as fast as he can, so he can dedicate more time to something higher and more meaningful on his priority list.

He has already identified one of his strengths as wisdom which includes finding new ways of doing things and thinking of different ways to solve problems. As a result, first Gary decides that he will sort all his paperwork into categories: action, archive, expenses, recycle, and shred.

When he is finished, Gary feels like he thrived on this challenge and after reflection, realized he created an environment where he performed a much better job than expected. Now he is both happy that his documents are more accessible when he needs them and that he has more time to do other tasks that are more enjoyable.

Some people can't relate to Gary and some people can. The truth pill to swallow here is understanding how to complete tasks by effectively engaging with your strengths. This is different for everyone. What works for Gary and lifts his performance might be different from what's impactful for someone else.

Take Wendy, for instance. Just like Gary she also has the task of filing to do so her job seems less repetitive. Unlike Gary, she uses her love of learning strength to lead the way. She decides to increase her knowledge of how to effectively file paperwork by watching an organization video on YouTube.

What she discovers is that she can eliminate clutter by scanning her important documents into an app called Evernote.[xii] This method allows her to capture documents, file them digitally, and they will be handy on all her devices. In the end, Wendy feels accomplished, and aligning her strength to her task has given her an opportunity to learn a new way to improve her process. She now can dedicate more time to other things at work that she prefers to do.

Everyone has preferences. This is true for what we do as well as who we prefer to work with. As we all know, there are some awesome people in our lives that we can't wait to see and love being with. There are also a lot of challenging people in our lives that we must deal with. So, are you wondering about how to bring all kinds of people together? Relationship crafting can help.

Relationship crafting involves how you can form or change up the type of interactions you have with others. This means that you try to work with others who will magnify or complement your strengths. On the flip side, it can help you use your strengths to deal with or block challenging people when you meet them. Unless you have lots of time on your hands, using relationship crafting as an approach will help you maximize your available time.

The goal is to assess which relationships are the most important to you and what kind of shape these relationships are in. You can do this by practicing a reflection of the people you interact with and how they affect you. Let's try.

Honest Reflection
Relationship Crafting

Rate Yourself (Low - High)	1	2	3	4	5
How often do you assess which relationships are most important to you?					
How well do you really know the people you live with, work with, or mix with?					
Do you really know how these people feel about you or how you come across to them?					

List the names of the students, work colleagues, friends, or members of your family that you should focus your attention on the most. Then rate your relationship. Is it in good shape? NO   YES

Keep in Mind:
Most people don't spend too much time thinking about these things let alone acting on them in any disciplined way. Even with the ones we love, we can be quick to judge, ill-informed about their possible motivations, and struggle to understand them beyond their basic surface level. In extreme circumstances, we miss the mark completely and see others for what we want them to be rather than for who they really are. But of course, it doesn't have to be this way!

Truth bomb: Some of your relationships may not be in a good place and bringing yourself to a place where you can think about them may be painful, frustrating, or make you angry. These feelings may lead you to avoid even thinking about things at all.

Now, before you fire someone, yell at them, or sign those divorce papers, it might sound crazy, but this is the best time to think about that person by looking at their strengths. Even though you may not be seeing much positive at the moment, they do have great things about them. You might start by considering what their strengths might be. You can also ask them to complete the VIA survey, so you don't have to guess.

After you consider their strengths, try to find a way through your negative feelings by reflecting some more.

Questions to consider include: *Do they have similar or different strengths to your own? How can you think about them in terms of what they are good at? What are their potential lesser strengths/weaknesses? How can their weaknesses help you understand them when they aren't at their best? Is it possible you are bringing out the worst in each other? Is your relationship broken or even dysfunctional?*

Relationship crafting recognizes that there is more we can do to understand another person's perspective, strengths, and weaknesses. If you look beyond what you currently assume about them, you may find something entirely different.

Besides a strength survey, there are other ways to spot strengths in others. Ask someone what they are good at or what they like to do. When people are sharing their strengths, they light up and come alive. The hardest part, when listening, is to suspend judgment and observe.

You can also observe someone. When people are using their strengths, their body movements will become more active. For example, some people might wildly gesture with their hands when they are trying to make a point. Other signs might include the speed and tone of their voice lifting from excitement and energy or their face showing signs of happiness. Their eyes might sparkle. Look for signs that they are clearly engaged, more energized, and seem like they are enjoying what they are doing. Focus on these qualities.

Alas, despite our best efforts to craft better relationships, we need to admit that sometimes it can be hard to get along and work with certain people. They may seem annoying or aggressive, and regardless of how you try. It may seem like every encounter with them is a struggle but avoiding challenging people for the rest of your life is unrealistic. Besides, you shouldn't need to. Enter cognitive crafting.

Cognitive crafting is a thought process that accepts the truth that when all else fails, even if you can't fix your tasks or relationships, you can shift your thinking. This approach makes situations more manageable and meaningful than they have been thus far.

You can use the knowledge of your own strengths and utilize your available resources to aim for opportunities that lift your mood. Resources might include items or people that can help you shift your thinking.

By changing your thinking, you can find or create more meaning about what might otherwise be seen as busy work or dealing with cranky people. This can help you recognize the link between specific tasks and big picture goals. Let's look at some cognitive crafting examples so you get the idea.

	Before Shift of Thinking	Resources	Cognitive Crafting
Person A	Changes bedsheets and cleans (strength = perspective)	Supplies	Makes traveler's journey more memorable and comfortable.
Person B	Prepares dishes and meals on time (strength = creativity)	Equipment	Create culinary artwork and uses food as an artistic medium.
Person C	Enters numbers and makes supply orders (strength = social intelligence)	Computer	Makes customers have a more enjoyable experience by being aware of their needs.
Person D	Edits articles for NASA (strength = humility)	Coworkers	Designs compelling content that generates interest for investors so the world can be inspired through air and space discovery.

Whether through task, relationship, and cognitive crafting, or all of the above, job crafting is a safe wager for a self-aware person since there are only benefits to getting more meaning out of what you spend your time doing.

Why Self-Aware People need Honesty

Imagine the uplift in work and life quality when authentic honesty becomes the norm. This is sure to change the realities of a less than ideal and often non-engaged workplace.

Honesty is a fundamental building block of a self-actualized person. The truth is that as an individual, you can't be what you can't see. Achieving the ability to be honest, with yourself and others, requires a great deal of work in self-awareness that starts with strength discovery.

Embrace Gretchen Rubin's words: "Accept yourself and expect more from yourself."[xiii] Identify, understand, and accept your strengths and how they set you and those around you up for success. This will give you the ability to live a truthful and fulfilled life.

You will experience challenges, but before you know it, you will get into the flow and be able to accomplish even the most undesirable tasks. And when with others, expect that we are meant to unlock the possibilities of our complex world and that collectively we can be successful.

Accept that honesty will lead you towards a world that cultivates capable humans working together in an authentic way to achieve awesome things.

Either you become the person who recognizes their potential completely and educates yourself on your strengths, OR you keep pretending that old practices and toxic workplaces are viable solutions to society's lack of success today. Please be honest about how you are preparing yourself and others for the future.

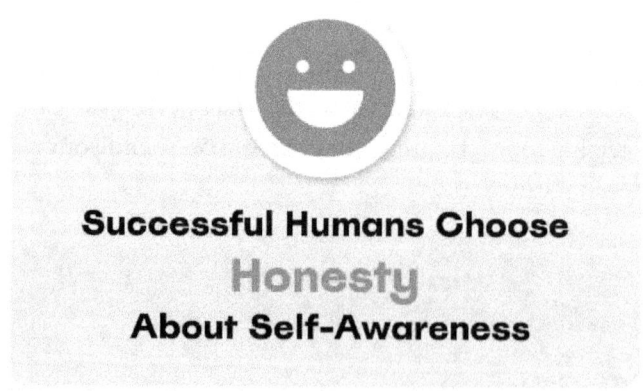

Part Two

"U"

Demonstrate <u>Unity</u> And Understand the Power of Teamwork

"It is the long history of humankind (and animal kind, too) that those who learned to collaborate and improvise most effectively have prevailed."
- Charles Darwin[xiv]

UNITY

Being self-aware and mastering your own strengths unlocks the ability and responsibility to do the same for others. This can even improve your tasks and relationships as a result.

Through teamwork, your actions can empower a group once you realize the potential they have. According to Simon Sinek[xv] what we need to tell people is, "You have capacity, you have strength, you have talent, you have ability. I need you to do more with what you have. We don't celebrate for what we've got. We criticize for what we don't have."

Creating a team's strength profile will help you clarify what strengths exist on your team and what strengths you may be missing. This is important when determining the team's ability to achieve mutual goals. You can do this easily by mapping each team member's top five strengths using the VIA character strengths survey.

If significant overlap exists in certain strengths, and a complete lack of another strength exists amongst the team, the group should assess what can be done to address this. Look at what needs to be achieved and which critical strengths are needed to do this successfully. If you are lacking the abilities and skills to achieve the team goals, one option would be to recruit a new team member who already has the needed strengths.

You can adopt a strength-focused approach to group work. One way is to develop a common language of strengths to keep everyone on the same page. You can also encourage all team members to speak up if there is a better idea. Either way, make sure that individual team members are working on tasks that align with their strengths and that they can help each other if things don't go as planned.

Don't forget about reflection. It is important to keep connected with how everyone on the team is feeling. If they are feeling they can do what they do best, if they are getting their work done, and if they are feeling energized, you know you are on the right track.

With this knowledge, welcome to the next chapter of your progressively stronger self. This is where you can now begin exploring what unity is and how it contributes to a far more human you.

Humans are wired for belonging, and when you are unified with others, the contribution that this has to your overall wellbeing should be taken seriously. Even the most reclusive of humans needs a connection to others. Loneliness is a killer and the power of the collective over the individual is shaping the narrative of the future.

Throughout our lives, we find ourselves in groups -families, friendships, work teams, or sporting groups we belong to. All of these can bring a variety of emotions such as exhaustion, exhilaration, and everything in between.

Ultimately, we all want to be part of something good that delivers impact and helps us get the best from ourselves. This is rarely done alone. But teamwork isn't always dreamwork and sometimes teamwork even sucks and feels hard and heavy. But expecting every exhilarating moment in life to be easy is unrealistic.

Success can't be achieved by always travelling on an easy street. Mastering the knowledge and skills required to effectively participate and achieve with others in groups has lifelong benefits. Let's explore.

Collaboration and Teamwork is the New Black

If you are on a team that you enjoy, chances are you look forward to seeing these people as often as possible and love achieving results with them. You feel like a connected member of a tribe that brings out the best in you.

Let's not sugar-coat it though; not all teams feel like this. That's exactly why developing your collaboration and learning skills is important. The result will be more of the great team experiences and less of the not-so-great ones.

It's a fact that teamwork is an essential requirement and not just a desirable quality for success in today's workplaces. The skills necessary to successfully navigate teams will become even more important in the future. The world of work that is growing in complexity requires people to work together to solve problems and innovate. These skills are among the most important in today's rapidly changing knowledge economy.

People have been talking about the importance of teamwork for decades. An old African proverb says. "If you want to go fast, go alone. If you want to go far, go together." In addition, we have heard things like, "It takes a village" or "Many hands make light work."

In the end, teamwork often boils down to two things: Step 1 – work on being your best self (as suggested in the Honesty section), and Step 2 – come together with others to achieve great things.

Innovation and performance are achieved collectively when individuals work together using their unique strengths and skills. The ability for you to perform at your very best, while also working together with other humans in effective teams, is where the magic happens for growth, success, and achievement. Put simply, we go further together.

Alone, you are limited by the edges of your own capabilities, beliefs, and practices. Even if you could do more or achieve more, you are unlikely to do it on your very own.

Teams should provide you with not only a strong sense of belonging but also with the willingness to go beyond your own boundaries. With the experience, perspective, knowledge, and the imagination of each team member, great ideas can manifest themselves into reality.

Not only can a team produce more than you can individually, but the power of the team can also make you, the individual, better. For these reasons, you should value your team and they should value you.

Just as teamwork skills are critical for success in the workplace, the same can be said of educational settings. Students who have a shared learning experience achieve higher academic results overall, as compared to those in an independent learning environment. As a result, cooperative learning or participating in learning activities and assessments that involve teamwork create a broader experience for the student. This translates to their work readiness as well.

Working with others helps you gain critical skills such as social awareness, problem solving, critical thinking, compromise, working with differences, negotiating, and influencing. Beyond school, the ability to work well with others is highly sought after as a transferable skill in a variety of career paths both professionally and in a trade. So next time you cringe and shudder about the idea of another group project or being slowed down by having to work with others, do yourself a favor and make the most out of the opportunity.

Okay, we've all had those nightmare teamwork experiences. Since we can't afford to give up on people that easily and since our future success depends on it, accept that developing teamwork skills is a must.

Moving from Me to We

Next step – moving the thought process from "Me" to "We." That's right, it's time to work on your ability to shift your thinking from inward thinking to an outward thinking.

In practical terms, it's important that people understand these thought processes in general. Inward thinking is "Me" focused. It's involves thinking about your own needs and wants, without necessarily considering other people as well. Outward thinking is "We" focused. It encompasses the idea that the goals of others are also important to you and form part of your decisions. Your focus is on group objectives and making decisions based on what is good for all because you enjoy being part of something that is greater than yourself. In addition, seeing others thrive gives you a buzz.

When you are in school, your thinking tends to be inward focused because you are curious about your own school outcomes. When you work, or indeed participate in life in general, your thoughts should have a balance of thinking about your own progression as well as what is best for the people you work and/or interact with.

An example is Mackenzie. She is an inward thinker that is a bit more extreme. She fixates a lot on her own feelings, circumstances, desires, and needs. She doesn't think about whether her behavior is appropriate with others. When other people have a really good idea, she rejects it because she didn't come up with the idea herself.

This could be her ego or perhaps she just lets her insecurities take over her relationships. Whatever the reason, her inward thinking will undermine any chance of her working well on a team, and this will become a problem for her if it becomes a habit.

If you are wondering, "Oh no, I think this might be me!" chill out because we have ALL been there. Just ask yourself if you have these thoughts and feelings on occasion, yet it isn't you all the time.

Perhaps you are still not entirely sure whether your thinking is more inward or outward? Pause to assess your thinking with the exercise below.

Ask Yourself These Questions

Do I immediately assume my way is better that anyone else's?	Yes	No
Do I usually think I am the smartest person in the room?	Yes	No
Do I always need my own wishes fully met before I say "yes" to something?	Yes	No

If you answered "yes" to any of those questions, then you are inward thinking. That's okay if you are willing to admit it and shift the balance a little more towards an outward thinker.

Living with an outward thinking brain is an asset to be built over time. The changes that this shift will enable in your relationships across the board can be extraordinary.

At the very least, people who practice "We" thinking notice more, are more connected to what is going on around them and can address excessive moments of "Me" and turn them into moments of "We" through small changes every day.

Essential relationship building skills and other benefits of "We" thinking are manifested when you:

- ✓ Regularly zone in and listen to understand when discussing viewpoints with other humans.

- ✓ Commonly succeed with, or through others rather than on your own.

- ✓ Actively and openly consider the ideas of others without judgement.

- ✓ Intently practice looking for positive gold nuggets in what other people say and suggest.

- ✓ Fully help others feel confident to share their ideas and thoughts with you.

- ✓ Naturally feel a sense of growth while building trust with others.

Without a doubt, "We" thinking is the steppingstone to one of the must have skills in the workplace today - In today's complex and often unpredictable world, the ability to work with others to solve problems is essential.

Great Teams Require Effort

Great teams accomplish magnificent things. Cool. You want some of that action for sure... but how do you know what a great team looks like?

A great team is more than just being "We" focused. Carl Larson and Frank LaFasto[xvi] studied the characteristics of great teams and wrote a book called *TeamWork* that details their observations of high-performing teams from a diverse range of backgrounds. Together, they analyzed a range of teams including the 1985 Mt. Everest Expedition[xvii] team and the space shuttle Challenger[xviii] team.

After reflection, they found ONE common and important factor that distinguished good teams from great teams - the willingness of team members to put in an extraordinary effort to help the team achieve its goals. Good teams do this from time to time, great teams live by this principle daily.

But consistent commitment and effort are something that even money can't buy. To have them, you must be willing to put in a huge effort over an extended period of time. And no one understood this more than the 1960s Green Bay Packers football coach, Vince Lombardi who said, "Individual commitment to a group effort – that is what makes a teamwork, a company work, a society work, a civilization work."

This concept is called "emotional commerce" and it enables a team to achieve far more together than is possible as individuals. But for this to occur, there needs to be a certain mindset displayed by team members. That mindset isn't automatic. It needs to be developed. Champion teams find ways to maximize their time together so they can achieve this.

Imagine a team of champion players, each highly developed as individuals and honest about their personal strengths, working together in unity, and getting the most out of one another. Everyone would want to be on that team. But make no mistake, there is a difference between a champion team and a team of champions. It may seem like a play on words, but it's a very important concept that helps explain why some teams fire and others misfire.

Champion teams have a clear game plan that involves hard work and determination. They also choose the right champion player for the right role. They do this so the team can perform their best and the team goals can be achieved.

In contrast, a team of champions looks like a whole lot of individuals running around playing to their strengths, but at times, oblivious to their teammates because they are focused on themselves. What's important is that all champions know what they are good at, play to their strengths, and keep developing their strengths overtime. BUT to flourish as a team, you have to know what makes your team even greater. You must work on achieving honesty and unity with the intention that you are willing to commit yourself to the idea that you can successfully work together.

You may be thinking: *Well, that's dandy in a perfect world, but what about a team member who just doesn't want to show up and play their part?*

We have all experienced frustration at a team member who isn't fully committed to achieving team goals or willing to work hard to achieve them. They are types of people who might be champions on their own but ultimately, do the team a disservice since they don't contribute to the big picture. Such as in the case of our example, Lou. Don't be like Lou. He only comes to work because he must and when he is there, he only thinks about how to be a champion by himself. You might have met someone like him.

Sure, sometimes things turn out okay for Lou. People give him high-fives on getting small jobs done. But for Lou, this is irrelevant because eventually this will catch up with him and he will find himself on his own and left behind.

As an individual, Lou needs to agree on a common team goal, focus on it, and be willing to work hard to accomplish it. Put simply, if Lou doesn't work on getting better at this skill, he will eventually struggle to connect and belong.

In other similar cases, when there is an obvious lack of connection between team members, it's essential to stop and figure out why. *Is the team goal clear? Do the team members understand it? Have they committed to it?* These issues will be addressed in future chapters. Whatever the reason, there's a lot your team can do to create the right conditions for a unified, committed team that performs effectively when they are willing to work hard together.

Teams are Multi-Dimensional

It is not realistic to expect a new team to perform at a high level when they first come together. High-performing teams have strong bonds. Don't go in and expect it to feel great from the start. This sort of unrealistic expectation will lead to disappointment, and you will likely give up before you get very far. Remember, forming a unified team takes time.

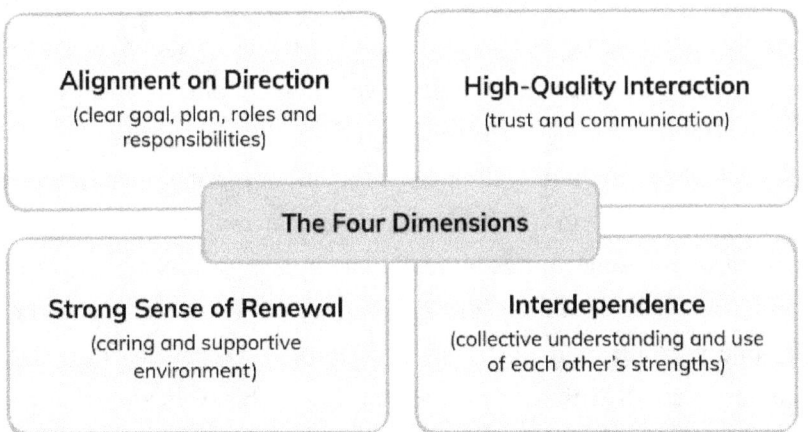

The immediate things to know are that you should be able to rely on your team. There are four fundamental dimensions that, in a semi-cosmic way, your team must journey through to effectively work together. As follows:

Dimension #1: *Alignment on Direction.* This dimension is about ensuring there is a shared vision about what the team is striving for. In other words, the "WHY" we are all doing this is clear for all. To have this, the team must establish a realistic goal, and it needs to be understood by all team members, so everyone knows the result they are working towards.

The team must also create a clear plan on how to get there, which all members must agree and contribute to. Don't skip over or rush through this first critical step. If you do, then you will be messing with the team's potential to reach awesomeness status. Without it, the team will lack clarity, direction, and commitment. This plan should include activities broken down into achievable "chucks" of work and assigned to team members. This will help ensure the work is done and create accountability for each task.[xix]

Ideally, alignment on direction should happen when people first come together in a group. It's good to start by getting the best, smartest people together to collaborate. This could be a group who already know each other or a bunch of total, hopefully reference-checked, strangers.

Either way, in this dimension, conversation between group members is typically polite and superficial as the individuals learn about each other and the work that needs to be done. It's a very "Hello. Nice to meet you." kind of conversation lacking controversy and drama. That's normal.

There are often high excitement levels about joining the new group and tackling the task at hand, but this excitement can include nervousness about working with people you don't really know or trust just yet. It's crucial to spend time in this dimension agreeing about the team's purpose that everyone is committed to. It can be helpful to "check in" on what each member wants to achieve as part of working in this team and what they see as the key goal of the team from their perspective.

Equally, when the team first comes together, it is important to create and establish norms. These will ensure the team can perform at a high level. It's essential that every member of the group has input to this but be mindful that not every person will feel comfortable speaking openly with strangers.

If someone is quieter to begin with, try not to let this frustrate you and lead to assumptions that this person doesn't trust you. It is helpful to agree on a way that people can have a say in private until they feel comfortable enough with the group to do it in the open.

To enable this, have everyone send their thoughts to one nominated person. This person collates the responses and shares them when the team next meets to see if they are all on the same page. The ideas and feedback can be discussed and agreed upon in the open. The team can then begin to establish norms by designing a social contract.

A social contract is a document that is written to encourage individual ownership of the group goals. It is an agreement on how everyone will behave themselves, and it is an opportunity to discuss how the workspace should function. Each team's social contract will look different, and if they are part of a larger group, if this is the case, their social contract responses can be combined to make one final social contract.

There are some essential questions that must be addressed when writing a social contract such as: *What are the non-negotiables? How should we treat the workspace environment? How do you want to be treated by your coworkers? How do you think your coworkers want to be treated by you? What are some examples of considerate behaviors? When there is a problem how should we act?*

Social Contract

Honesty ✓✓✓✓
Set Weekly Goals ✓✓
Respectful ✓✓✓
Empathy ✓✓
Growth Mindset ✓✓
Time Management ✓✓
Feedback ✓✓✓✓
Clear Expectations ✓✓
Kindess ✓✓
Self Advocate ✓✓✓

This can be designed by using a large piece of chart paper or whiteboard. Once the social contract is discussed and agreed upon, a final copy can be written up and everyone on the team can sign it. For instance,

Social Contract

As a coworker, I promise to have a growth mindset and be respectful of my time and working space as well as others. I promise to set weekly goals for myself and manage my time to complete tasks so my coworkers can give me feedback. I promise to have empathy for and show kindness to others because that is what I want from my team. "Lastly, I promise to follow clear expectations from my team leader, advocate for myself, and be honest with my team if I am struggling professionally or emotionally.

I _____ , have read and understand the social contract. By signing this document, I am in agreement with the above contract and will follow its guidelines to the best of my ability.

Signature: _____ Date: _____

After norms are established, the next requirement for a high-performing team is to build strong relationships. This happens in **Dimension #2:** *High-Quality Interaction.* This relates to how team members interact to build trust and openness with one another. This ensures each person can contribute their best. Beware that this requires effective, honest communication.

It also requires a pre-agreed upon approach to addressing potential conflicts when they happen so the team can keep progressing. A key determinant to high-quality interactions is openness to ideas from everyone. It doesn't always mean that the idea someone has will be progressed, but everyone knows that the idea will be heard and respected. This means all the people working together know their ideas won't be shot down nor will they be ridiculed. This results from team members who trust each other.

This is called psychological safety. This stuff is real, tried, and tested! Google conducted a two-year study[xx] of its staff and found that the biggest factor to high performance in its teams, in fact, double any other factor, is psychological safety.

Stephen Covey's book, *The 7 Habits of Highly Effective People*[xxi], seconds this concept. He suggests that, "Without trust, we don't truly collaborate; we merely coordinate or, at best, cooperate. It is trust that transforms a group of people into a team."

Ideally, high-quality interaction happens after the group has met a few times. In this dimension, often, its normal for members to be pushing boundaries and expressing their different working styles. For the team to be exploring ideas and approaches, they must be meeting frequently and checking in on progress toward their agreed-upon plan.

If the team hasn't reached the high-quality interaction dimension, even after meeting a few times, it's worth pausing and finding out why. *Has trust been built yet? If not, what is needed to build trust? What more can be done to get there? If yes, what aren't team members leaning in and contributing to idea generation?*

If the team has reached the high-quality interaction dimension, you can expect to observe some animated discussions and potential conflict in opinions here. Be cautious and acknowledge some people might not agree with the group's goal.

Also, be aware that some groups never exit this dimension, as people can be fierce and confrontational. Instead, they break up and go their own ways. Given they still need to achieve the desired outcome, individuals are likely to revert to working on their own and throwing things together right before the outcome is due. And you guessed it, the outcome will be disastrous. Don't let this be your fate.

A source of potential friction in this dimension could develop if roles and responsibilities within the group haven't yet been made clear. There may be confusion over who is doing what. Maybe more than one person wants to lead, for example, or the objectives of the group are misunderstood. Often, it's helpful to appoint an observer and/or mediator who has permission from the group to intervene when required.

In the high-quality interaction dimension, healthy tension is important for the group to resolve its issues and can be used as an opportunity to reconnect with what the common goal is. This is also a chance to strive for collaboration and discuss what may be causing disagreements and how they can be resolved together. Keeping an open mind, good listening, and a willingness to compromise are the qualities you must possess to collectively move out of this dimension and into the next one.

Dimension #3: *Strong Sense of Renewal.* This gem is achieved by helping team members feel safe to take risks (and potentially fail) in the pursuit of the team goal. What they will experience in this dimension is a sense of "renewal" because their team will rally around them without judgement and help them "bounce-back" and overcome when they stumble. Team members are energized because they feel they can innovate, learn from each other, and bring in new ideas.

The point is people should feel comfortable enough to contribute opinions, feedback, and solutions. This is called an *inclusive environment.* The more diverse and inclusive your environment is, the more people will feel like they can contribute and thrive in it.

For team members to feel safe to take risks, it requires the team to show genuine care and support when things don't go to plan, or mistakes are made. This is sometimes referred to as "having each other's back" and yes, you need to support people during hard times.

It's in this dimension that roles and the big personal conflicts have been resolved, so the team's focus turns towards a task. Clarity is gained about what needs to be done and the detail of the work is clear.

This is where you get to taste of the sweet nectar of effective collaboration. Even when the work gets hard, and it will, you will find yourself admitting that it feels pretty good when the team is unified. You should be checking in with each other, bouncing ideas off each other, or feeling comfortable to just download frustrations.

You may observe social norms beginning to develop such as catching up socially or taking breaks together at an agreed time. Although there can be an occasional slip back into alignment on direction, in general, this is where you get that fuzzy feeling that there is a firm sense of "team" amongst the group because you are building on each other's strengths.

Over time, setbacks become less and less frequent with fewer adjustments needed when processes don't seem to be flowing smoothly. As support improves, the wonderful vision of the last stage comes into focus.

Dimension #4: *Interdependence.* This is about each team member knowing, valuing, and depending on each other's unique talents and strengths and knowing that when they rely on one another, it's a secret weapon rather than an anchor.

In this dimension, unified teams thrive on diversity by recognizing and celebrating everyone's individual strengths as the team achieves important milestones together. These celebrations help motivate the team to keep going.

This works best when individual team members determine their own unique strengths and then collectively determine group strengths and weaknesses and how they complement one another. When a team reaches its peak performance, they can operate effectively regardless of challenges that come up. You know you are on the right track if you feel connected and part of "the tribe."

Covey talks about this in his book as well. He says, "Life is, by nature, highly interdependent. To try to achieve maximum effectiveness through independence is like trying to play tennis with a golf club."

If any of these four fundamental dimensions of teamwork are not in place, teams will struggle to achieve their full potential, experience dysfunction, and fail to reach their goals. You may need to adjust accordingly and bounce back and forth between the stages as needed. These pivots are essential as is frequent assessment of which dimension your team is currently in.

It should be noted that when people start working together, the character or culture of the team will reveal itself. This is called team dynamics, which is a fancy way to describe how your team interacts with each other. As predicted, a strong, unified team will take you much further than you ever expected.

This was the case in 1992 with the roster of the US men's Olympic basketball team. It had some of the greatest players in the history of the sport to date. We are talking about basketball legends such as Charles Barkley, Larry Bird, Patrick Ewing, Magic Johnson, Michael Jordan, Karl Malone and Scottie Pippen.

In the end, it was evident that just bringing together superstar players doesn't guarantee success. In their first month of practice, the "Dream Team" lost to a group of college players by eight points in a scrimmage. Scottie Pippen responded to the loss by saying, "We didn't know how to play together."

So, what did they do? They considered the four dimensions, adjusted, and learned how to play as a team by understanding how to combine their strengths. As a result, the team not only won the 1992 Olympic gold, but also dominated the competition, scoring over 100 points in every game.

Considering the four dimensions works. *Don't believe us?* Think of the game tug of war. If the team is not all pulling at the same time, in the same direction, they will lose the game. This is alignment in direction. But that's not the only consideration to success.

In tug of war, the team also needs to communicate that they have a "We" mindset and they intend to win. This high-quality interaction can be achieved if they trust that everyone is trying their best.

If the team keeps getting pulled over the opposition's line, team adjustments need to be made. The team needs a strong sense of renewal that, through collaboration, they can discover more effective methods of working in unison or pulling in the same direction.

The team needs to understand the strengths and contributions that each team member can bring to the team for success. To achieve this, they must ask themselves questions such as: *Who is the biggest or heaviest member to anchor the team? Where should each member be on the chain to achieve maximum strength? Who motivates the team to succeed by showering them with encouraging cheers? How should each member be arranged to meet a winning outcome?* This is interdependence.

The key takeaway is that unified teams are multi-dimensional and need: alignment on direction, high-quality interaction, strong sense of renewal, and interdependence.

Unity Can still Exist between Different People

Ever imagine how stress-free life would be if everyone was like you? Coffee is just the way you like it. Responses that don't make you frustrated. Seems blissful. But no. Reality check! Life is full of different types of people, and you need to learn how to work and achieve together.

If your group is too similar, things might be conflict free and easy, but the result might be one-dimensional, unimaginative, or biased. This is the reason navigating diversity is another essential need to maximize people towards success. But the road is bumpy, so buckle up.

As discussed, having diversity on a team is valuable. However, with it comes differences, and with differences, comes the possibility for conflict. As we know, some conflict is essential to pushing boundaries, forcing the creation of new and sometimes better ideas. BUT if it gets out of control, conflict can not only get in the way of performance, but it can also destroy teams.

Trust us. The ability to work with people who have different strengths than yourself is something you need to do on a regular basis. **Truth Bomb:** Your exposure to differences, depending on how you grew up, might be lacking.

In our younger years at school, we are often surrounded by people very similar to us, and from among them, we choose the friends we want to spend our time with. This changes a bit after high school where we might be exposed to a broader range of people, but we still have choices about people we want to stick with.

Careers are different. Once you get a job, you can expect to work closely with people who are very different from you across a range of aspects. This includes differences in racial or cultural backgrounds, religion, age, sexual orientation, education level, socioeconomic status, and tea over coffee drinking preferences.

These people will have differing opinions that may be based on very different outlooks than your own. You must learn to work with all kinds of people especially if you plan to lead them.

No one can achieve success, whether it is in our social circle, business, or studies, if relationships between people are strained. Instead, relationships must be nurtured and sustained. This requires the ability to recognize and be open to other people's differences rather than jump to judgement when someone doesn't feel, think, or act the same way you do.

If you want to feel unified in the time you spend with other people, it will require you to respect others' differences as you would want them to respect your own. This is the starting point for real collaboration.

Malcolm Forbes once said, "Diversity is the art of thinking independently together,"[xxii] to address how successfully navigating and leveraging diversity requires more than just bringing multiple voices together for a conversation. It requires a culture and mindset that helps people thrive by encouraging them to both be themselves, while at the same time, be a person who aims for togetherness and collaboration.

When we feel empowered to think independently, psychologically safe to express our true thoughts and ideas, while actively collaborating as one team (the essence of interdependence) great results follow. In other words, people enjoy feeling like they are respected for their independent thinking regardless of if the group chooses their ideas.

So, is there a perfect mix of people? Well, they say variety is the spice of life! While you can't guarantee a perfect mix, a combination of personalities and cultures can create one hell of a recipe for an awesome team. It can be hard and even frustrating, but to have this, you need to deal with different personality types.

It's a little naïve to assume that any person and any personality type can work together by just coming together. If you want an ineffective team, ignoring personality differences is the way. But if you want balance and success, pay attention.

You don't want a team that is full of highly analytical individuals with no one who thrives on action. We call this analysis-paralysis. In other words, you don't want too many thinkers who have a strategy that looks impressive on paper but never gets executed.

If you want to understand how people can operate or who works best together, apart from their collective strengths and weaknesses, learn to identify personality types and behavioral styles. When you have this insight, you can then decide how to appeal to their style, adjust your own style, increase their effort, and get the best results. It's all about awareness and balance.

There are many different models and theories about classifying personality types and behaviors. You can do your own research if you'd like to find your own preferences.

The DiSC Model

Dominance
Relates to how you control different situations. It is the extent to which someone is decisive, adventurous, direct, a risk-taker, assertive, and self-reliant.

Steadiness
Relates to how you interact with others. It is the extent to which someone is optimistic, persuasive, emotional, charming, sociable, and impulsive.

Ways people express the four key behavioural styles

Influence
Relates to your temperament. It is the extent to which someone is consistent, cooperative, deliberate, patient, loyal, and composed.

Conscientious / Compliance
Relates to your process and attention to detail. It is the extent to which someone is accurate, analytical, tactful, sensitive, systematic, and precise.

The DiSC Model is a fascinating starting point. It's a personality test that assesses the extent to which people express four key behavioral styles - Dominance, Influence, Steadiness, and Conscientious (or compliance).[xxiii]

Although personality can vary in different situations, we all use these behavioral styles to some degree to achieve our goals and all people have a preferred style that they naturally default to the most. If you are wondering how a person can understand the viewpoint of another person and how they might react in the context they are working in, meet our example couple, Joan and Fred.

Joan is a high-dominance person who is decisive and direct and willing to do what is needed to get the job done. Fred is high in conscientious, meaning that he can be quite sensitive and needs things explained to him while also needing to understand the detail behind things.

This is why Joan must be aware of how her abrupt style can feel rushed to people like Fred. Her style might get in the way of them being able to work together cohesively on projects that involve research.

Another example couple might be Jack and Sue. Jack is strong in steadiness and Sue is low in steadiness. They both know this because they have taken the time to understand each other. Because of this awareness, Jack might notice Sue struggle to stick to deadlines which impact project timelines.

Jack could reach out to Sue and suggest they work together to come up with a plan and stick to it. He knows that his behaviors of optimism and persuasion mean that he can really help Sue stay on track.

If you understand your teammate's behavioral preferences and potential cultural differences on a deeper level, you can find a way to bridge the gap. You can use this understanding as a secret weapon for success when forming balanced teams and leveraging this for great outcomes.

Remember, your goal is to have an interdependent team that is a good mix of all personality types and will therefore, be effective in progressing toward goals. Be on the lookout if you feel like your team isn't generating great ideas and solutions.

Here are the things to consider when you are trying to form an interdependent team with people who are different from you:

If you have a team that is too heavy with one type of personality or set of strengths, be aware of how this might be derailing team outcomes.

Too many dominant people will probably lead to clashes and a lack of well-considered or tangible outcomes. If your team lacks dominance, they may struggle to come up with innovative ideas due to low risk-taking.

Too many steady people will mean the team may be too agreeable with one another (often called group think) and won't challenge enough. If your team lacks steadiness, they might struggle to stay focused, on track, and on schedule.

If your team lacks influence, they may have amazing ideas but struggle to get buy-in from your audience.

If your team lacks conscientiousness, they may have great ideas but could fail to execute successfully with accuracy.

Basically, if your team is lacking in one or more personality types, be aware that this will likely impact team effectiveness as the team may get stuck on certain tasks or goals.

Considering these things will help you maximize your people and navigate differences in a positive (open-minded) way. Enjoy.

It may seem like some people sneak drinks from the fountain of positive vibes, but really, when people can see differences as opportunities, they can unlock new possibilities for their personal growth and the effectiveness of their team.

Understanding how to form an interdependent team means embracing several truths that accompany it and underpinning it all is empathy. This is a must have if you want your progress to translate into tangible outcomes.

Truth #1: Before you open your mouth, remember, people are full of complexities. It is not just personality types and cultural backgrounds that influence us, but also our moods and emotions. Sometimes people are wearing a set of cranky pants, and it can be helpful to remember you don't always know what someone else is dealing with or going through.

Don't try to force others to think like you, because not everyone should be the same! You can't control other people, but you can control how you approach them, perceive them, engage with them, and how you choose to communicate with them.

Truth #2: Be as flexible as possible when it comes to your approach to others. Try and keep an open mind towards them free of assumptions. Try to adapt your communication style to suit the needs of other people. If someone has an introverted personality type, try to talk to them one-on-one rather than in a group setting.

Same goes if someone is dominant. They are more likely to say what they think but may take up a lot of the talking time, sometimes aggressively. Give them a chance to express themselves and make sure they can share their ideas, but be careful that they don't railroad.

Importantly, resist the tendency to assume people are being intentionally difficult. People are simply who they are sometimes. The chances are, they are as frustrated with you as you are with them when things are not working. They are making decisions based on their unique personality, cultural background, and previous experiences. Your challenge is to adapt to them. Never try to change people. It is always easier to adapt to your own style because the only person you can somewhat control is yourself.

Truth #3: Avoid negative labeling of others like the plague. Respecting differences starts with an open mindset that reserves judgement and automatic negativity when something doesn't align to your own opinions or views.

We all know how easy it can be to call someone annoying or difficult when they frustrate the hell out of you. Don't judge people who communicate or act differently than you. Instead, try pausing and attempting to get to the reason behind your annoyance.

Ask yourself: *What is driving your need to assign a negative label to that person?*

Are you an extrovert and the other person is an introvert? Do you judge them for their lack of willingness to say what they think and find yourself not trusting them as a result?

In reality, some introverted people are more reserved about saying what they think, particularly in big, very public ways. Other questions to consider include:

Are you an introvert and find yourself really put off by the extroverts in the team that are loud and crave attention?

Do you find yourself judging them as being bullies or egomaniacs when they may be saying what everyone else is thinking but are too afraid to say?

Bottom line, there is no right or wrong answer to all of this. Next time you meet or have to work with someone who is frustrating you, just try to think about your personality and why it is different from theirs before you attach a rude negative label to them.

Truth #4: See people objectively, not personally. You don't have to like everyone you meet or work with, but it sure helps if you find a way to see them positively and find the good things about them. We ALL have good things in us.

Let's say you meet a somewhat irritating guy named Saul. You find yourself so annoyed by him that you can't face being in the same room, let alone hanging out with him or even being his friend.

Perhaps try looking at him objectively. Instead of thinking, "I like X about Saul, but I don't like when he does Y," consider, "Saul is just Saul, and I will take the time to get to know him better so I can understand where he is coming from."

Having this positive mindset is essential to building trust and being able to work with relative strangers and achieve results quickly. You literally can't thrive in today's working world without this.

Truth #5: If Truth #4 fails, focus on the task, not the person. You may find it easier to change a behavior or thought towards an activity or task versus your individual thoughts about a person. The way you do this is by focusing on the common goal. You may have different views, backgrounds, and communication styles, but you can all be united to get the job done.

Try to focus your energy on what's needed to get the task done rather than your individual differences. Don't let social issues cloud your decisions about what's going to get the job done and what's best for the team.

Truth #6: Don't be afraid to ask questions so you can understand and embrace differences. Sometimes it seems easier to avoid people or ways of thinking that are different from our own. Try taking the opposite approach and inquire why someone is not working the same way as you are.

Taking a moment to understand someone else's perspective and behavior can challenge your assumptions in a good way and even help you see things in a different light. Maybe your own way of thinking and working needs adjustment. Either way, be brave and stay open.

Truth #7: Respect yourself and others by picking your battles. Respecting yourself isn't always about standing your ground, sometimes it's about knowing how and when to pick your battles and letting your empathetic and patient side shine through. Letting the small things go, for example, differences of opinion, means you can concentrate on getting your work done without taking on unnecessary stress.

Respect your time and energy. Respect your need to prioritize things that really matter. Stay balanced. If you find yourself endlessly pouring energy into something or someone, check in with yourself and ask if it's worth all the effort.

Without Conflict it is Difficult to have True Unity

Okay! You now know about the stages of teamwork, strengths spotting, behavioral styles, and working with people who are different from you. Before you move on, learn that part of being unified is celebrating teamwork moments when you can.

Celebrating successes involves taking a small break to boost morale and for folks to process their achievements. It's a great way to break up the normal vibe and remind your team of why they do what they do. Besides, it's never a bad idea to take stock of how the team's efforts are making a difference.

Speaking of differences, teams will inevitably have their ups and down. Heck, even successful people have their obstacles. And when this happens, you need to know how to recognize the causes of conflict. You also need to know the difference between healthy and unhealthy conflict and how to stop things turning toxic. In the next chapter, you'll read about how to manage and respond to conflict, so keep your hat on.

First things first, contrary to popular belief, you can keep things positive by having the right sort of conflict. We do not need to fear conflict because not all conflict is bad. Conflict is pretty much inevitable when you work with others, and healthy conflict is essential for highly effective teams and their ability to innovate.

Developing the skills to identify good and bad conflict means you can increase the leverage of the positive impacts and minimize the negative. You need to understand what conflict is and how it comes to be. A *conflict* is more than just a disagreement. It is a situation in which one or both parties perceive a threat regardless of whether or not that threat is real.

Conflict arises from differences that can be both large and small. It occurs whenever people disagree over their values, motivations, perceptions, ideas, or desires. This sort of conflict arises when people feel that their core values are being challenged and/or are at risk.

Sometimes these differences appear unimportant, but when a conflict triggers strong feelings, a deep personal value is often at the core of the problem. It may start out as a simple disagreement based on differing points of view. Often, these disagreements can be resolved quickly. However, sometimes people do not move in a positive direction because disagreements can escalate into a negative response.

Unresolved differences can also turn into an unhealthy conflict. This will damage relationships and hinder goals. Understanding differing viewpoints involved in a disagreement is a key factor in helping to resolve conflict in a healthy way.

Healthy conflict may sound like such an oxymoron, but it simply means the conflict is constructive. This kind of conflict incites disagreement but doesn't encroach on people's basic respect for one another, so no perceived threat exists. It's a sign of trust and security that people can instinctively share their thoughts and opinions with others who make them feel comfortable and psychologically safe.

To lay the groundwork for healthy conflict practice facilitating it by creating a space where you feel free to speak up because you know you are being listened to, heard, understood, and validated. This kind of environment encourages people to be confident, lean in, and express themselves even with opposing points of view. This is critical for generating creative ideas.

The other added benefit is that you can discover the potential barriers for the group. This will create a "safe" space for conversation. Even if this space is seen as conflict, it tends to bring bottled-up issues to the surface so they can be resolved. This kind of conflict is healthy because it often leads to better discussions and decisions.

Unhealthy conflict, on the other hand, can be characterized as having disagreements that lead to negative impacts. These can include hostility, loss of trust, and inability to work together effectively. Imagine feeling stressed, dissatisfied, anxious, and withdrawn. This type of destructive behavior can quickly become a part of your team dynamics and make high performance and team success impossible.

Unhealthy conflict should be avoided and can rear its ugly head through gossip, undermining, and divisive side-taking. These things do not ever support a productive team environment so do your best to avoid cultivating this type of energy.

Conflict can trigger strong emotions. So be aware that if you aren't comfortable with your emotions or aren't able to manage them in times of stress, you may struggle to resolve conflict successfully.

People respond to conflict based on their perceptions of and emotional response to the situation, not necessarily to an objective review of the facts. Our perceptions are influenced by our life experiences, culture, values, beliefs, general health, and mood.

But as hard as it can be to lean into conflict, avoidance is the enemy of progress. If conflict is ignored, it will continue to fester, impact stress levels and ultimately, team health and individual's well-being.

"Conflict," as Nate Reiger, author of *Conflict without Casualties* suggests, "is simply the energy created by the gap between what we want and what we're experiencing."[xxiv] Sounds positive when put this way, right? It can be, but it needs effort and careful consideration by team members to ensure the conflict isn't mismanaged.

If you don't want to cause harm to your relationships, consider healthy conflict as an opportunity to strengthen the bond between people within teams. Understanding the human response to conflict takes work and careful effort to ensure discussions stay respectful and as positive as possible, without becoming too comfortable and losing their potential for innovation.

How to Manage and Resolve Conflict

To be unified and increase the good times, you should be aiming to maintain a healthy balance of constructive difference of opinion and resolution of disruptive negativity or unhealthy conflict. Techniques, that will be discussed in this chapter, exist to help you deal with conflict in a positive way.

While taking note and action on all of this, just make sure you understand that everything will not get resolved instantly. Sometimes shit will really hit the fan and an unhealthy conflict will break out despite your positive mindset. In this case, freaking out, shouting, or conversely withdrawing isn't really a great choice. And yes, it is still possible to turn things from a negative to a positive.

Eight ways to turn a negative situation into a positive-constructive conflict:

#1: *Acknowledge the conflict.* This must happen before it can be managed and resolved. As you acknowledge it, make sure you read the room by looking at your team members' body language, facial expressions, and tone of voice. This can be the first sign of conflict brewing and can say more than just the spoken words.

Before you speak, pause and take a breath. It might also be appropriate to ask for a quick break to reset with the intention to come back and resolve the issue together.

Take the time to gather your thoughts understand what is frustrating you and why. Form a clear, honest, positive non-judgmental "I statement" by thinking about why you are feeling frustrated.

For example: I feel _____ (state the emotion you feel) when _____ (tell what caused the feeling). I would like _____ (explain what you want to happen instead).

When you make this statement, your intention should be to diffuse friction and foster engagement. Cooperation will allow all your team members to begin the process of resolution of the issues. Your desire to win and be right can't be greater than the want to resolve the conflict and move forward.

#2: *Listen to all perspectives.* To move on, you should seek to understand where each person is coming from. That means everyone needs to make an "I statement."

#3: *Agree to communicate.* The most important thing for conflict resolution is for everyone to keep communication open and honest. To accomplish this, speak your mind in a helpful way.

Work to communicate assertively yet positively. Assertive communication is a great skill to have. It means getting your message across honestly, clearly, and directly, without being threatening. By taking this approach you're telling the other person how you feel without being angry, hostile, or ignoring your own feelings.

Be careful though, the other person might not be happy about your feedback. No one likes to be called out on their behavior. By being assertive, without being confrontational, you will have a better chance of both of you having a mutually acceptable outcome.

An example of someone who assertively communicates well is our friend Ella. She is a kind woman, and most people find her pleasant to work with. Occasionally Ella lets her frustrations get the best of her and she sometimes finds herself getting aggravated with people and being quite curt in her responses. This was the case when she met Greg who would continually check his phone or look around when she was talking with him.

These days, she better understands how being assertive can be helpful and has developed the ability to use "I" statements to help her respond. She might say something like (in a helpful rather than condescending tone, of course), "When you look at your phone or look away when I'm talking, Greg, I don't feel like I have your full attention. I would like you to participate more."

#4: *Be mindful of emotions.* For many people, conflict is difficult and challenging. It can lead to negative emotions which can contribute to stress or a reactive state response. These emotions can also make it more difficult to use constructive responses to address the conflict.

#5: *Show empathy.* Using your understanding of differences as well as your empathy can be powerful. Ask questions to understand the underlying cause of the other persons emotional response. For example, if they have sweaty palms and a fast heartbeat, they might be feeling anxious. Deadlines might make them feel this way, and as a result, their behavior might be to yell at people.

#6 *Compromise.* This can be an effective method for managing conflict and differences. There may be situations when agreeing to disagree on some points is the best option. Anyone who has been in heated political conversations knows you can't make someone change parties overnight. Compromise is usually required when there is this type of disagreement.

#7: *Be respectful.* Stop worrying about being liked or about liking everyone. You can't please everyone, and this is true in your personal life and in the workplace. If the team in which you are working is productive and everyone feels respected, it's okay if everyone is not the best of friends. Aim to be kind to each other and make respect be your group's priority.

#8: *Be adaptable.* Allow yourself to be flexible when you handle changing conditions, personalities, and stresses. Remember, it's not about changing people to eliminate differences that cause conflict, it's about managing these differences to extract the positive and minimize the negative.

The mutual acceptance of differences increases the likelihood of a productive resolution to the issues at hand. Remember, pick your battles.

Whether your team is new or been together for some time, by spotting strengths and by understanding behavior styles, a diverse mindset, and constructive conflict, you can maximize the great team experiences. You might even look forward to seeing the people you work with.

You can either be the type of person who loves achieving results with people you feel like you are connected to or the type of person who feels tribeless and filled with regret for not trying to understand how people can bring out the best in you. You are not perfect, and neither is your team.

All you can do is try to remember your collective goal is to achieve success. To do this, teams must be unified.

Successful Humans Demonstrate Unity and Understand the Power of Teamwork

Part Three

"M"

<u>Maximize</u> Potential and Communicate with Impact

"When you start communicating to change people, you leave a lasting legacy. You profit from your impact, not in spite of it."
- Dr. Michelle Mazur[xxv]

MAXIMIZE

Do you know the most effective way for young people to collectively make connections, develop relationships, build trust, share information, and make progress?

Say it with us now- the world needs to learn more about communicating with impact so you can maximize your and your team's potential. Indeed! Whether or not you want to embrace this truth, communicating with impact is essential in life, and you need to learn how to do this or consider collective success unattainable.

If you are one of those people who argues with the notion that success can't happen when certain people work together, then start by embracing that fact first because there is most certainly strength in group dynamics. So cut yourself a slice of this humble pie. Heck. Even color it if you'd like, but remember always:

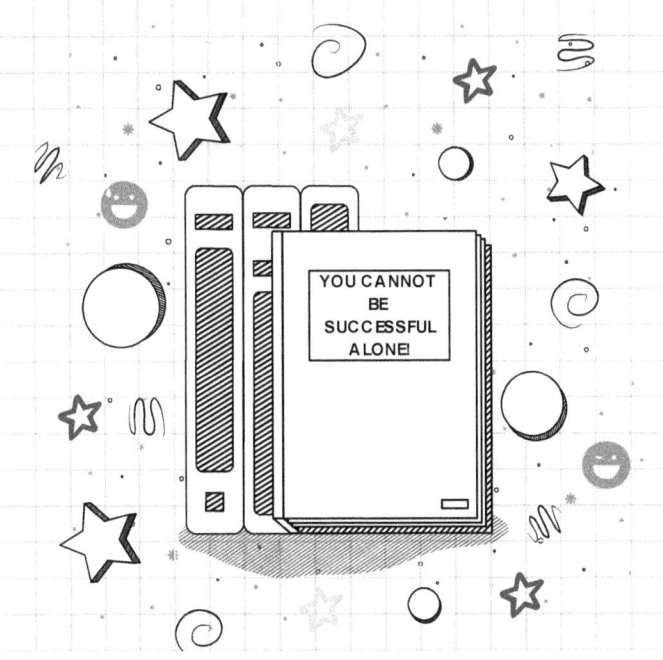

Whether they are family, teachers, mentors, or trusted friends, just about every day you will engage with a variety of different people. To be successful, you will need to learn how to build these meaningful relationships. This can be achieved by communicating with them in authentic ways.

Authentic communication is a necessity and people who can communicate this way are the kinds of people who get shit done. They have inquisitive conversations, they fill meetings with lively discussions, and you can see evidence of their impact in everything they do - whether it's a presentation, a work bulletin, or praise from the mouths of other leaders.

Contrary to what many believe, authentic communication is not an innate skill, but rather, one that must be developed. You can practice this skill by being self-aware, through reflection, and by interacting with other people. Your action plan should involve maximizing your potential and the potential of others. As a result, you will become comfortable discussing problems, requesting information, and influencing other people on your team.

If authentic communication is so important to maximize your potential and the potential of others, why isn't everyone good at communicating this way?

Well, there are several reasons your team might be struggling with communication. But before you get all bent out of shape that you or someone else is lacking the skills needed to make an impact, in the next chapter we will look at some of the main causes.

Getting to Know Your Barriers

Before we begin, you should know that for you to communicate with impact you must first get over the fear of getting it wrong. The reasons behind fear may include looking bad, being criticized, feeling judged, suffering rejection, feeling insecure, losing friends, or just having the fear of blanking out and forgetting what you wanted to say in the first place. These *brain farts* can be understandably scary, but they are not impossible to overcome. Practice, preserve, and practice some more.

The reality is that being a good communicator involves a lot of practice, preservation, and is hard to achieve. Mastering it means having lots and lots of "being out of your comfort zone" moments. You will probably hate these moments, but the more of them you have, the better you will become better at communicating well with others.

Being confident when you are communicating is not something anyone achieves at birth. These skills are learned by putting yourself out there and gaining experience talking to people. Only then can you be on the road towards adjustment and improvement. The key is to know your barriers: what they are, what they might look like in practice, and ways you and others can overcome them.

There are six barriers to communication: technological, physical, language, cultural, psychological, and organizational.

Technological barriers of communication emerge when people either don't have or aren't using digital tools effectively. We can see what this might look like in practice by observing someone like Kelly. She curses under her breath all day because her computer constantly crashes. An easy way for her and others to overcome this is by upgrading or replacing technology as necessary.

Derrick also suffers from a technological barrier, but his case is trickier. He frequently uses short form communication methods like texting or chatting to get his message across. He doesn't realize that his avoidance of face-to-face conversations is obvious. This is a huge barrier that will require a no excuses approach.

One of his excuses might be that this approach is convenient or perfectly suitable for some situations, and he'd be correct with that one. He is incorrect, however, if he overly relies on this communication mode. This method can hinder him from building the required trust and rapport needed to maximize the outcomes of the people he is trying to communicate with.

There is no context in text messages. Complex issues are rarely resolved that way as intention can get lost in translation. Generally, this sort of communication should only be used with people you know well or if someone has advised you to use this method in urgent situations as the best way to contact them. Avoiding phone calls and in person communication is missing a lot of the ingredients needed to build trust in a relationship.

If the person Derrick is communicating with doesn't know him well, then his digital message can read as if he is insecure or that he is using this method out of laziness. A digital message seems efficient and quick for the sender, but the experience for the receiver may fall short. To overcome this, the people who work with Derrick can develop rules for how and when to use specific communication channels.

Physical barriers to communication can occur when people are too far away, such as when working remotely. Gloria, for example, is experiencing a physical barrier, and this is evident when she complains often about working remotely without strong systems in place to keep people connected.

One way to overcome this barrier is for Gloria to adopt and maintain different ways she can connect with her team. Perhaps she could be provided with training to communicate virtually. She could also be provided with a stipend to explore workspaces that include built-in tools for digital teams.

Language communication barriers can occur when someone speaks English as a second language or when someone struggles with translation. Depending on experience, people might not even realize they are creating a language barrier.

Janis, for instance, is a team leader who doesn't know that her team is struggling with the differences in her vocabulary. She thinks when she says things like, "Let's pepper it in, synergize efforts, or swing for the fences," that she is being helpful.

In truth, her communication efforts often lead to frequent misunderstandings, complaints of lack of clarity, and disagreements around multiple interpretations of her message. So how can she overcome this? To start, Janis probably needs to check back with her team regularly to see if she communicated effectively. Once she recognizes her messages are getting lost, she can try to adjust her own language and encourage her team to use clear, concise language that avoids slang, jargon, and figurative language.

Cultural communication barriers stem from people who have differences in their values and social norms. In practice, we can see an example of this panning out with Linda and Bill. They come from different backgrounds, but they both want to feel included. Bill sometimes makes what Linda feels are inappropriate jokes and now she avoids him as much as possible. As a result, she complains about his behavior, and they can't communicate effectively.

To overcome this, Bill and Linda need to participate in regular sensitivity sessions that are conducted by inclusive culture experts. This is where they can be educated on the missteps in other cultures. These sessions can be paired with one-on-one conflict resolution meetings as needed to address ongoing concerns.

Psychological communication barriers occur when certain individuals feel unsupported and undervalued. Edward, for instance, has a phycological barrier. He is constantly absent and lacks engagement because he feels when he tries to communicate with others, he can't rely on them to provide him with the resources he needs to be successful.

Edwards needs to be offered opportunities to collaborate with others or he will never overcome this barrier. Feedback can take many forms, such as daily meetings, open office hours, or anonymous surveys. Either way, Edward must be encouraged to have open and authentic communication.

The last communication barrier is *organizational.* This barrier forms from a lack of understanding of a business structure and the individual roles within it. It affects groups or teams of all sizes and it happens when people are unaware of or do not fully understand an existing way people should communicate.

We can see this in action by looking at situations like Christine's. She frequently contacts the wrong individuals for specific insights. Other people often get upset when vital information is lost or delayed somewhere along the chain of command or when the chain of command is not followed, and a lot of people think it is Christine's fault.

To overcome this organizational barrier, there needs to be a clear structure that includes roles and contact information. This needs to be widely available, easily accessible, and included in new hire orientations or induction programs.

There is a time and place for all channels of communication and finding the right ways to overcome barriers is an absolutely critical skill to develop. Failing to do this may mean your communication doesn't achieve its desired outcome.

Now that we have raised your awareness and identified potential barriers you might have, the next step is to understand the different ways we can communicate with intention.

Time to get your skates on...

The Four Communication Types

There are four main communication types that can be used to get your message across. These will help you maximize the potential of yourself and your team.

The first is *Verbal Communication*. This includes the words coming out of your mouth and the words you write.

The second is *Para-verbal Communication*. This is the *way* you use your voice. It includes volume, pace, pitch, punctuation, and how you place emphasis on the words you are saying.

The third is *Non-verbal Communication*. This is the way you use your body language and other physical cues even when you are not speaking.

The last is *Visual Communication*. It can be seen in the form of pictures, graphs, and animation. This form of communication often sparks emotional responses and mastering it can often help you say what you need to say quickly.

Now that you know the four communication types, it's time to decide on the right communication approach for whatever situation you are in with another human. Depending on what's on your plate, you might want to choose one or a number of these approaches in combination for communicating your message. Choices might be limited by current situations, but if you have the choice, take time to consider the most appropriate way of getting your intention across.

As an example, let's say you want to deliver a simple message quickly. In this instance you have a choice. For example, especially outside working hours, go with an email, a form of verbal communication. Choosing to use verbal communication only in this situation is being informative in a simple form.

In a more complex situation that involves hearing someone else's opinion, you would probably want to opt for a phone call. This means you're choosing verbal communication and para-verbal communication. Good for you.

All right, now let's try serious conversations that are sensitive or important. Do you want to discuss an issue or get a promotion maybe? Then face-to-face is most appropriate in this case. It means you are choosing to use verbal, para-verbal, and non-verbal communication. If you have graphs or charts to present, you've added visual communication as well.

Okay now moving on to when you do not have a choice. Maybe you are applying for a job, and you need to submit your resume via a job search website. Face the facts and use verbal (in written form) communication here.

You might choose to include visual elements to elevate your resume or provide examples of your experience. This can help set you apart from other applicants, but it should be approached cautiously as inappropriate visual elements might send the wrong message.

Knowing how to effectively deliver your message is half the battle in effective communication with an intended positive impact. Surprisingly, in spoken communication, a speaker's words are only a fraction of what is needed to deliver his/her message, intended or not.

A study from the late 1960s, by a professor named Albert Mehrabian, found that when you are speaking, the impact of your communication is divided into 7% for *what* you are saying and 93% of *how* you are saying it. The *how* can then be further divided into 38% for tone, pace, and pauses (para-verbal) and 55% (the vast majority) for body language and eye contact (non-verbal).[xxvi]

A lot happens when we talk. We send out signals simultaneously - things like volume, speed, pitch, posture, hand movements, excessive scratching, eye contact, the list goes on and on.

How the information receiver reacts to the way you communicate and what they choose to do afterwards depends on you successfully combining these four main communication types. Understand that your signals can work for or against your message.

If you are aware of the signals you are giving off, fantastic. But the truth is, whether they are painstakingly obvious or subtle, they can be used to emphasize and amplify your message. Or they can be used as contradictory statements to the listener. Be aware of this as well. For example, when you are being dishonest, you might say one thing, but your body language may indicate an entirely different message.

Our non-verbal signals are often instinctive, and some people find them not so easily faked. These are generally more indicative of a person's true feelings. On the flip side, if you are aware of this as the receiver of messages, you can now weed out a few negative people in your life, which is always nice.

Either way, this is why it's so important to be aware of and interpret all the signs and cues that you might be sending and interpret those you are receiving. It's also important to work out *how* you will respond based on your understanding of all the elements of communication. This takes time to master.

Which brings us to the next part of this section. Let's talk about structuring and crafting your message, regardless of the method of communication you use.

Planning and Crafting Your Message

Say it with us now, *breathe in learning to be a good communicator, breathe out planning and crafting your message.* This is the needed thinking of a maximizer.

Get ready. You are about to embrace the maximizer mindset of Antoine de Saint-Exupéry, the author of *The Little Prince*,[xxvii] who once said, "A goal without a plan is just a wish."

In other words, don't just wish good communication to happen, make it happen through some savvy planning and preparation. After all, it's a requirement.

Planning is a word you are going to hear a lot from us. And rightfully so, as your level of planning will directly influence the success of all the communication you will ever have as a human. Our approach to planning involves shaping the planning process. The biggest questions to address are:

What are you trying to achieve and How will you structure the communication for maximum success?

Sure, if you'd like, you could fly by the seat of your pants, go off the cuff, ad-lib, wing it, or have a let's see how it goes approach to communication, but if you are not willing to risk the outcome, you better do some prep first.

When you do, remember this: there will be a direct relationship between how much effort you put into preparation and the likelihood of your success.

If you are cringing at the thought that every single encounter you have in life will require an extensive communication plan, relax. Not all communication opportunities are as important as one another, and we understand that your time is limited.

Speaking of time, you should know that the amount of time spent on preparing for types of communication will depend on a few things: Importance, Formality and Circumstances. All these words have simple definitions, and you should understand them if you want to maximize your chances of success.

Importance is when you consider if whatever you're doing means a lot to you. If it does, then you should spend a lot of time doing it. Think about how much you want something, and then invest the equivalent amount of time to prepare.

Formality is considering who you are communicating with and what their requirements of etiquette, regulations, or customs are. People or companies that expect a higher level of formality also require more preparation.

Circumstance is the last preparation time consideration. Sometimes circumstances do not allow you much if any time to plan. Some conversations happen last minute, making planning impossible.

What is important is that you weigh these factors: importance, formality, and circumstance and then decide how much effort should go into preparing. Then use some common sense in deciding. You probably don't need to prepare for a chat with your friend, but you probably do need to prepare for a chat with your boss, especially if you are asking something important.

When weighing these factors, allocate time for planning things like writing important emails and even more time preparing for something like a public speaking engagement. You should always start the decision process by beginning with the end in mind. This is where you think about the kind of outcome you want to receive from your audience and the kind of impact you want to deliver:

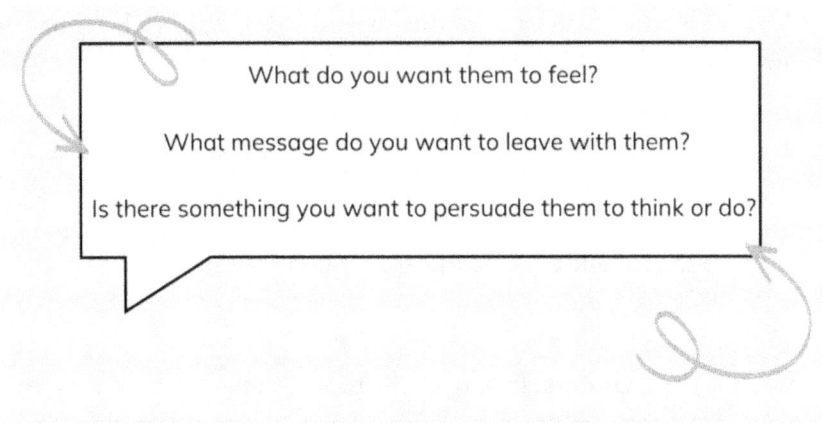

What do you want them to feel?

What message do you want to leave with them?

Is there something you want to persuade them to think or do?

Once you have this all sorted out, if you want to deliver an impact in your communication efforts, you need to clearly define your key messages.

Think about what you are trying to achieve and the clear messages you need to share to get that outcome. Take the time and do this properly.

Make sure you consider the structure of an argument by choosing three to four main points. Don't throw too many ideas into the conversation. Be disciplined and keep it simple. Less is more. Consider the points as adhering to a personal thesis; this is the foundation for building your message in an impactful way. The main points you identify will become the backbone of your communication opportunity if you understand your audience.

If you don't understand the needs and wants of the person (or people) who are receiving and interpreting your message, you can't possibly craft an effective communication opportunity that will create a lasting connection and impact. Consider who your audience is and what they may or may not already know. A word of caution: don't assume your audience knows the background details like you do. Equally, if they are experts, don't talk to them like beginners who need all the background information.

Think about their preferences, their style, and base your approach on what you know about them. This can involve making decisions such as using technical or simple language, being casual or formal, and being bold or subtle.

Think about your audience and keep these thoughts in the front of your mind for deciding things like appropriate structure and formats (such as emails, reports, presentations, storyboards, videos, interpretive dance...you get it). As a resource, you can use this suggested AUDIENCE framework that summarizes the above points.

<u>This is a useful tool when you are thinking about the audience and their needs:</u>

A – Who are the **Attendees** that you are communicating with? (It could be one or more people).

U – What is their **Understanding** of the topic – how much do they know and understand about it already? Are they beginners or experts?

D – What **Data** do you have on who they are – gender, age, education level, cultural background?

I – What **Impact** do you want to make? Do you want them to be moved? Uplifted? Motivated to perform a specific action?

E – What **Environment** will your audience be in when you deliver the message to them?

N – What is the **Necessary** approach to get the desired outcome? (Decide how to format the communication – written, in-person, remotely etc.).

C – What appropriate materials might you **Create** to support the message you are delivering?

E – What is the **Expected** outcome from the audience? What would they consider a valuable use of their time when receiving your message?

After clearly defining your message and understanding your audience, work on crafting your message to be interesting, believable, and understood. This is a must. It will require you to do some research to support your key points with interesting and relevant information, anecdotes, or facts.

In writing, authors do this to provide their readers with a voice of authority but doing this really helps people absorb your message. When you do this, remember to be choosy with what information you use so you can avoid evidence overload.

Be confident in your research. It should give you a good grasp of what you are talking about when you are trying to deliver an impactful message.

This confidence will help you worry less about *what* you are saying so you can focus more on *how* you are saying it. Consider it an investment in being a successful communicator. It will also help you believe in yourself.

You can build your confidence by remembering that every good communication opportunity has the same three key themes: gaining attention, delivering the information in an engaging way, and ensuring retention of your audience.

Attention is sometimes good and sometimes bad, but either way, it can always be gained. This is where you must do something to spark your audience's interest. Maybe it's a shocking statement or a funny or emotional anecdote, but it should always get to the heart of your issue and be delivered in an engaging way.

When it comes to *gaining attention*, we all know how painfully obvious it can be when we listen to someone who doesn't care about what they are saying. Their body language gives it away every time. Instead, they can utilize communication opportunity strategies in their message delivery. Where relevant, they should use personal stories to really stress their key points.

Personal stories gain attention since they help listeners connect emotionally to what you are trying to say. In writing, this persuasive technique is called emotional appeal. It allows the reader to trust the author enough so they can believe in their message.

Next up is people who can *deliver messages in an engaging way*. They recognize the details humans use to maximize their intended impact. This can mean considering things like visual elements. When used correctly, they are very effective in communicating key points since they deliver a lot of easily understood information quickly.

Pro Tip: You need to balance talking about facts and data with talking about personal stories.

Facts and data can be valuable. They can help you present a strong argument with an approach based on solid evidence rather than guesses. They can also be used as displays to support your areas of strength.

Some people prefer to stick with personal stories while others might feel uncomfortable and think you are an over-sharer. They might judgingly say, "Why is this person disclosing so much personal information?" Maximizers say, "forget them." Some people think aluminum foil hats protect them from bad vibes too.

The truth is, when you use stories, narratives, and anecdotes to engage your listeners, your audience can better connect with what you are saying, and this will keep them interested and engaged. This builds a rapport with your audience quickly. If the stories are relatable enough, they allow for an easier and genuine connection with people.

Storytelling will declare that your message is planned with the intention of making connections with your audience. Additionally, when you harness the power of storytelling, believe it or not, you are helping your audience to retain information. If planned correctly, your stories should be honest and vulnerable accounts that pull your listeners towards your carefully crafted message. This will be elaborated on in the next chapter.

Ensuring retention of your audience is the last component you will need to master when it comes to planning and crafting your message. To begin, retention involves how your audience commits to remembering your message after they read, view, or listen to your content.

We all retain information in different ways. While there is no hard and fast rule about this, the consensus about retention is to make sure your audience sees, hears, and does something. According to the National Highway Institute, "Adults retain approximately 10% of what they see, 30% to 40% of what they see and hear, and 90% of what they see, hear, and do."[xxviii]

To obtain the seeing and hearing part, make sure you keep your message clear, interesting, and include visuals. As far as the doing, you can encourage your audience to participate by asking a series of questions, by using a polling tool, or asking them to take action such as recommending that they turn on Twitter so they can respond to your message in real time.

After all this talk of planning and crafting, don't panic if you have a situation where it's not possible. It happens. Sometimes you get put on the spot and your guard is down. If you are in a situation where and you can't ask for some time to pull your thoughts together, you might feel some anxiety creeping in. This topic will be explored later in the book.

For now, focus on the idea that the more you practice and improve your communication skills, the more confident you will become in these types of situations. Also let's make sure we really have a grasp on the power of storytelling before we deal with anxiety.

Effective Storytelling is Always in Fashion

Maximizers believe that storytelling is a far easier way for humans to absorb facts and figures. They know their words have the potential to make a positive impact because they understand that, through connection, we can make information more memorable.

Think about the last presenter that you really listened to with deep engagement. It's most likely that they told you a personal story that you really connected with. So why are stories so effective?

Storytelling is human. It's a unified way that people can connect through sharing thought-provoking events, interesting information, and honest personal experiences. As an engagement strategy, it helps people place an emphasis on key ideas that are needed for successful communication.

As children, stories, such as fairy tales, can have a lasting impact into adulthood. They can influence your decision making, be unique, bind people together, or transport people to a different place.

For tens of thousands of years, people have been telling stories, and the best ones have withstood the test of time. They don't just deliver information; they make us feel a certain way about ourselves.

Did you know that when the brain is exposed to stories, it can cause the listener to feel like they are experiencing something for themselves? We never miss the opportunity to geek over a quick neuro-science lesson, thanks for humoring us.

When you communicate using facts and information only, limited parts of your brain get activated, to be more specific, the frontal lobe and the cerebral cortex. These are the language and memory processing parts of the brain. This is where your brain controls reasoning. It's also the place where people decode words into meaning.

Once the brain hears facts and makes sense of what has happened, that's it. The brain parks this information and moves on. However, when people are being told a story, not only are the language processing parts of our brain activated but also the areas responsible for hearing, listening, visual processing, and verbal comprehension.

These activities happen in the left temporal cortex if you're curious. Regardless, stories activate a much greater portion of the brain, and this broadens the connections people will make to your message. The result is they experience the information, rather than just consuming it.

If you learn how to be a good storyteller, you are not only embracing the beautiful brain science behind it, but you are selling your message. That's the art of storytelling.

Shane Snow and Joe Lazauskas, authors of *The Storytelling Edge*,[xxix] claim that "Good stories surprise us, they make us think and feel. They stick in our minds and help us remember ideas and concepts in a way that a PowerPoint crammed with bar graphs never can." This couldn't be truer.

It might be true that some people have a natural "gift for gab" when it comes to storytelling, but they are diamonds in a pool of ordinary stones. For the rest of us, it is a skill that can be developed for those willing to put in the effort.

To begin practicing this skill, you should be aware of what great storytellers want to achieve. Above all, they want to successfully draw their audience in, keep them captivated, and keep them listening. How can you do this?

Before you have a moment when you wish you paid more attention in language arts class, rest assured we aren't about to shove a bunch of terms down your throat. Instead, we recommend you simply use two the key elements of good storytelling. Your story should be relatable and relevant to the listener.

First, your story should be *relatable*. No one wants to hear a story about your delusions of grandeur when they are just starting out. People want to hear a story that benefits them in some way or that they can relate to.

One way you can make your story relatable is by sharing data, through storytelling. Data is an incredibly powerful way to make what seems like an endless amount of the tedious and overwhelming facts seem more meaningful. When people tell us they love data, we don't believe them. People don't love data. They love what the data provides, and that is a relatable good story.

For example, let's say Carlos needs to put together a presentation for a health conference on the ways people can avoid contracting malaria. He finds a lot of data about the subject and, among all his facts, he finds one that tragically shows that in 2017, there were 435,000 deaths from malaria globally.

Even though that's a big number, and you can see how relevant it is to what he is communicating, it may have no relevance to the people he is sharing it with because they are not affected by malaria. In other wards, they can't relate to the topic.

To make the data more meaningful, he might want to tell a story instead about a particular family who was torn apart by malaria and its effects in 2017 when there were 435,000 global malarial deaths. In that story, he can give examples of how disease can be avoided. This is a topic all people can relate to. He can make his message more emotional if he includes questions like, "What if it was your family member?" And then BOOM. Suddenly, the data he is sharing becomes more personal, less abstract, and relatable on a human level.

Secondly, your story should be relevant. This means your story should be appropriate to the current time, period, or circumstances. Let's say Lenin is at the same health conference as Carlos.

Lenin is trying to put together a presentation on ways health care centers can improve patient health. If this is the case, it's probably not a good idea for Lenin to use visual aids from the 1930s to the 1950s. This is when doctors lit up the pages of cigarette advertisements, and it has been confirmed that smoking will not improve your health.

Lenin can also not get to off topic by talking about when he was in third grade and he won the spelling bee. Likewise, mentioning how he likes singing in the shower is also not a good idea. Unless Lenin can connect his examples to the topic, he should avoid all information that is not relevant to his story, or his audience will be confused.

Effective storytelling involves using relatable and relevant stories as secret weapons. This is how maximizers communicate a meaningful message that delivers an impact.

At this point, we have talked about spoken verbal communication through stories. Next up, we will include how maximizers verbally communicate by choosing words that can deliver a message with impact.

Be an Excited Word Nerd

Maximizers are word nerds. They get excited about words because they know the words they use have a considerable impact that can either be neutral, positive, or negative.

For example, if you needed to spend the weekend at my place and I told you I live in an apartment or a house, you probably feel neutral about this. However, if I changed my words and told you I live in a beautiful mansion, that would have a positive connotation, and you might be dreaming of my indoor pool and my lavish in-home theater. The same goes if I described my place as a messy shack; you'd leave the conversation thinking of all the negative things associated with my crib.

There are loads of communication opportunities for word nerds that can have an impact. For example, the written form could include exams, essays, emails, instructions, CVs, reports, blogs, letters, whitepapers, and directions are some ways. The same is true of spoken form.

When it comes to communicating through writing and speaking, you should intend to be a word nerd. To begin, first accept that words are powerful.

The meaning of our words drives our behavior and ultimately creates our environment. Their power arises from the emotional responses of the receiver when they read, speak, or hear them.

Don't believe us? Try saying the word "fire" at a barbeque. Then try shouting it in a crowded theater. Now read the word silently to yourself. What you'll get are three completely different but powerful reactions.

In written form, the receiver does not have access to other cues, such as tone and body language, so word choice is everything. Some people like writing better than speaking. They are, after all, in more control of what they say, since they can reread what they write before they send it.

The downside, of course, is that they don't get to use their non-verbal cues to help deliver the message, and they sometimes must wait some time before receiving feedback. Emojis have become increasingly popular in written form because of this, but we would not advise using them in formal writing.

For this reason, so much emphasis is on the words you use, so make sure they help you land your intended message before it goes out to the public. It helps to take a moment to think about how the recipient will interpret your message when it is received.

Secondly, word nerds accept that, in the larger sense, there is an actual relationship between written communication and verbal skills. Take spelling and grammatical mistakes, for example.

Have you ever read an email with a ghastly typo and just thought to yourself, "This person is obviously a moron!" These kinds of things are non-negotiable in writing. Be careful. Poorly written communication can be frustrating for the reader and potentially damaging for the author. What you write represents who you are and what you are trying to say when you can't be physically present.

Having good writing skills allows you to build trust and communicate your message with clarity and ease. You might also want to check for your structure and flow.

It helps to read your writing aloud because this forces you to verbalize what you have written. Pretend you are reading your story to someone else; this approach will help you pick up issues that your eyes would otherwise skip over. On a side note, this is also a good way to proofread.

Maximizers avoid using overly big words and too much jargon. They don't think it makes them look smarter, and they know it increases the risk of their message getting lost in translation. They do not want to leave their readers feeling confused, and neither should you.

It's nice to include some visual information to break up all your words and sentences -- plus it can strengthen your message. This will be covered in a later chapter. For now, just know that readers will appreciate the reinforcement of all the key points.

Pro Tip #1: "Readability calculators" tell you how easy your writing is to read. Companies like Grammarly offer them as addons. or you can write down this link, use it on your computer, and it will analyze it for you: https://goodcalculators.com/flesch-kincaid-calculator/

In Word, you can turn on readability stats (1) Go to "File," then "More" and "Options." (2) Select "Proofing." (3) Under "When correcting spelling and grammar in Word," make sure the "Check grammar with spelling" checkbox is selected. (4) Select "Show readability statistics."

Pro Tip #2: Try to remember that you should be aiming for an educational reading level that is slightly lower than your audience. In education, this means teaching with a respect to your reader's lexical level.

Remembering that words are powerful and that there is an actual relationship between written communication and verbal skills is something successful maximizers do. *But who do word nerds hang out with?*

Find Great Feedback Nerds

Word nerds meet your new besties - the feedback nerds. Be open to them and they will help you improve. Ask them for feedback because they are the people you trust and whose writing style you admire. This is such a glorious way to improve your verbal and written communication skills!

If you are lucky enough to have feedback nerds in your life, take them in, and get comfortable asking them for help. Don't torture yourself wondering if your message is on the right track. Hang out with feedback nerds for a while, and you'll find out.

You can't just have a new bestie without being a good friend yourself. At this point, we are here to remind you that communication is so important that it's worth going the extra mile. This means learning how to be thoughtful about who you are communicating with and how your message makes them feel. The feedback nerd can help you with this since they will tell you how your message makes them feel.

A good feedback nerd will tell you that it is your responsibility as an effective communicator to consider how your behavior affects your audience. Although sometimes brutal, they offer their advice in the form of suggestions that can help you make your audience respond as you intended.

If you intend for your audience to feel empowered, you should maintain a positive attitude when communicating. Even if you are surrounded by a lot of cynical people, they don't need another cynical point of view.

In response, feedback nerds will tell you that positive attitudes sell ideas. Believe in what you're saying and writing. Do this with conviction and an open mind. Remember, confidence builds confidence. And all that fearing rejection and self-protecting hoopla, dump it!

Trust us. You need to hear what your bestie is trying to tell you. But proceed with caution. You will not always agree with their suggestions.

In those times, listen and thoughtfully respond when you and your feedback nerd disagree. Why the hell should feedback nerds help you if you are just going to get defensive?

To avoid getting defensive, never start a feedback conversation with "You're wrong" in response to someone's opinion or ideas, even if this is how you feel. This applies to all situations: work, study, and in life, of course. The trick is to remember that even though you are receiving a constructive response, you can present a counterargument to convince your feedback nerd otherwise.

In any case, it's certainly not nice to make your feedback nerd feel belittled. If you do this, they, and your audience might start to resist your ideas.

For example, if bestie says something that deep down you feel is unbelievably ridiculous or even stupid, try saying something like, "I see where you are coming from. Maybe we could do XYZ…" Instead of just shutting down their ideas.

No friend, classmate, colleague, or person likes to feel dismissed, so never ignore your feedback nerd. If you hit a wall in your argument, or there are all sorts of misinterpretations in your message with them, we recommend reflection, clarification, and questioning.

In writing, allowing peer editing to happen with your first draft is recommended. It's okay to show your feedback nerd your message as a work in progress. Don't wait until it's finalized when it's harder to mentally let go of what you already have on paper. This way you can avoid a whole lot of re-work.

The more you understand why another person feels the way they do, the more you will be in control of making good decisions while you are communicating. This is the reason why good feedback nerds are not sensitive to misunderstandings. They know that word nerds need to recognize and embrace different ways of interacting and communicating.

Tony Robbins once said, "To effectively communicate, we must realize that we are all different in the way we perceive the world and use this understanding as a guide to our communication with others."[xxx]

Which is why we think it's important to mention that great feedback nerds, who communicate effectively, operate in "receive" mode as well as "broadcast" mode. That means they listen or read actively and speak or write with intention.

They also have the skills needed to deal with different personality types and cultural differences. For instance, let's say feedback is given to a person from a western culture. They tend to prefer to be told things in a blunt, direct style. A feedback nerd would know that this might create a cross-cultural misunderstanding since in many other cultures, a direct communication style can be considered rude and insensitive. This is why in most conversations, feedback nerds avoid slang and idioms. They tend to be culturally specific.

Speaking of culturally specific, a feedback nerd would tell you to watch your body language, since certain gestures can be positive in one culture and highly offensive in another. Even every day gestures may not be safe. For example, across the Middle East, a "thumbs up" gesture is considered rude.

Another example is in Australia, the US, and UK, a head nod of up and down indicates agreement or acknowledgement, but in Greece, Bulgaria, and Albania, nodding means "No."

Are there more culturally specific body language gestures you can think of?

Respecting how your message makes people feel, by embracing suggestions, and by dealing with differences, is a responsible way you can be a good communicator thanks to your feedback nerd friendship. With this knowledge, you also need to recognize that different situations will require being flexible with your communication.

Adapt What You Say

When challenged, it's important to remember that the only person you can control is yourself. Sometimes, you might need to adapt your own communication style to suit that of the other person.

For example, as mentioned before, if someone is an introvert, they have a more reserved personality type. You can be adaptable by trying to talk to this person one-on-one rather than in a group setting. Likewise, if someone is more dominant, group settings will be fine, but watch that they don't take over and shut others out. Everyone should have an opportunity to share their ideas. Regardless, never try to change people.

It's easier to adapt your own style rather than to force others to be or think like you. People can change themselves if you model positive actions first. Plus, they will appreciate your courtesy, respect you more, and respond in kind.

In written communication, adapting will include omitting information your readers do not need or making sure key facts are not missing. You can also provide examples or change the organizational structure of your message.

Oral communication gives you even more options to adapt your listeners or to the situation. Maximizers demonstrate adaptation by being aware of *how they say the things they say.* In other words, when they speak to people, they "read" their voice in addition to listening to their words. These are those para-verbal skills.

We talked about them earlier and they make up a whopping 38% of how impactful your communication is going to be! This includes pitch and tone of voice, speed and rhythm of your words, and use of effective pauses. You can't speak without using para-verbal skills and they go hand in hand with verbal-skills. The conversation breakdown illustrates this.

When we speak, our message it received like this:

55%	Body language, eye contact, etc. (non-verbal)
7%	Words
38%	Voice, Tone, Pauses, etc. (para-verbal)

Para-verbal skills include changing your tone and inflection of voice. They contribute significantly to how your message is being received. As an activity, try practicing by saying the word "No" using different tones. You might discover your para-verbal skills might need to be adapted if your tone of voice indicates sarcasm, anger, or fear, rather than affection or confidence.

Although a little more challenging, this can apply to writing as well. SEE ALL OF OUR CAPITAL LETTERS IN THIS SENTENCE? BET IT FEELS LIKE WE ARE SHOUTING AT YOU! Yes. Capital letters are a written way of expressing tone.

Speaking of shouting, volume is a key factor when speaking. Too soft and you may seem too modest. People will think you lack confidence and conviction. Too loud and you may blow your listeners away and make them feel like you are yelling at them or are domineering. You can adapt this too. *How?*

Try varying your volume between soft and loud. This is called having volume variety and it helps create interest which holds your audience's attention. It's at the extremes of volume where you want to draw your emphasis to be.

Here's what we mean. If we put volume on a scale from 1-10, with 1 representing speaking very quietly and 10 speaking very loudly:

Between 6 - 8 on the scale	This volume is considered active
Between 3 - 5 on the scale	This volume is considered moderate
1 and 2 and 9 and 10 on the scale	This volume is considered powerful

Adapting your volume includes using the active levels of voice volume (6-8) for moments in your communication that you really want to emphasize. This helps grab the attention of your listeners. Then for impactful moments, try loud and proud (9-10) or drawing your listeners in to a secret with whispering (1-2).

The pace of your voice is another para-verbal tool you can adapt. It will play a big part in how your message is received. If you're speaking too quickly, like the legendary fast talker John Moschitta from the 1980s (look him up on YouTube for a laugh),[xxxi] people will find it hard to understand you, keep up with what you are saying, and may even feel overwhelmed by your presence.

Equally, if you are speaking too slowly or ssss----llloooooowwwwl---llllyyyyyy your audience may feel bored. As a result, what you are saying will lack impact, and you may even seem a little condescending.

Adaptation means finding a natural, medium pace, with the occasional use of slow and fast words used to create interest at the right moments and a pleasant flow. This might take some practice, but after a while, you can find your sweet spot.

The last thing maximizers know about adapting their communication is the power of the pause. Pausing is one of the most underutilized secret weapons for communicating effectively. A well-timed pause, otherwise known as having a "golden silence" moment, can make a big difference to delivering your message.

Often people don't pause because they just want to get their message out. Resist this urge even if you are feeling nervous. Pausing for two to three seconds can: create... dramatic... effect!

A bonus is that pausing also lets you rest and solidify what you are going to say next. Pausing is both a rest for you and your listeners.

Using, varying, and adapting your para-verbal approach can really help lift your chances of success when it comes to getting your message across. When it comes to communicating with impact, embrace adaption. Above all, spend the same amount of time improving *what* you are going to say as you do planning *how* you are going to communicate as you do improving *what* you are going to say.

The Secret Non-Verbal Ingredients

Maximizers know that variety is the essence of great communication! They also know that what they are going to say isn't the main game. They consider all the ways they communicate even when they aren't speaking.

As discussed, para-verbal skills are important, but don't neglect non-verbal signs and cues to consider. In fact, much of what we say (remember that 55% in the conversation breakdown?) isn't communicated through words.

Like painting a picture, a non-verbal cue can speak a thousand words. So basically, you must master the skill of having a grip on your body language because believe it or not, you can send and receive messages without using words.

It's all about how you act when conveying a thought, feeling, or an idea. People respond through physical gestures, posture, and facial expressions. In writing, *italics* and **bold** fonts can be a way to place emphasis on language.

Think about it. If you asked us how we feel about our current education system's lack of focus on career readiness, and we looked at you with angry faces flailing our middle fingers in the air, you'd get the message, right?

The exception, or perhaps confusion, would be if you were from some Middle Eastern countries where it's considered appropriate to point using the middle finger. Again, cues can take on many forms and may be interpreted in multiple ways by different people, especially across cultures.

Given that body language is often instinctive and not easy to fake, it generally reflects a person's true feelings. This is particularly true as demonstrated in the previous paragraph when people are trying to speak with assertiveness. It also happens when people are trying to speak with conviction, passion, nervousness, impatience, or lack of belief in themselves.

Many people look like idiots. They don't even know it. Your body language tells your listeners many things about you.

It can indicate whether you care, if you are being truthful, and how you are listening to them. When your body language matches the words you are saying, your message is elevated to the next level of impact.

The opposite is true when your words don't match what your body is doing. Imagine someone saying "I love you" while they are chasing you with a knife, for example. The outcome of this situation is likely to cause confusion, disengagement, tension, and mistrust.

If you can get your body to reinforce the words you are saying, you have a much better chance at making an impact with your communication. Body language can support, strengthen, or weaken what you are trying to say.

Intentional body movements and gestures can play a big part in communication as well. Repeating movements, for example, can help you strengthen what you are trying to say. Imagine if you saw someone repeatedly point at an object. Naturally, you would think they are trying to show you something important. You can do this too.

Author and educator, Peter Drucker once said, "The most important thing in communication is hearing what isn't said."[xxxii] Keeping this in mind, we think it's also a good idea to make complementary movements and gestures that will reinforce your message. For example, a smile emphasizes warmth and appreciation.

Physical contradictions like the crazed, love-struck idiot with a knife, can undermine or negate what you are saying, and they provide mixed messages. So, you will want to avoid carrying weapons and doing things like smiling when you are giving bad news.

You'll also want to avoid things like looking at the ground while saying you are interested in what someone has to say. Physical substitutions, however, can be a great replacement for saying something. For example, a nod, shake, or hug can be used instead of saying anything.

Body Language Cues (with notes) to Remember:

Facial Expression	Whether it is happiness, sadness, anger, surprise, fear, or disgust to name a few, your face is the mirror to your mind.
Body Movement and Posture	Consider how people perceive the way you sit, walk, stand, or hold your head. The way you move communicates how you are feeling. If you stand tall, others assume you are confident.
Gestures	This includes things like pointing, nodding, waving, or using your hands. Remember these might mean something different across cultures. Watch out for excessive use of these as they can be distracting.
Eye Contact	The way you look at someone can communicate many things, including interest, affection, hostility, or attraction. Really looking someone in the eyes will help you create a connection, but try not to stare or that could make things super awkward. Stick with four to five seconds.
Touch	Sometimes referred to as haptic communication, this is the way people interact via the sense of touch. Examples include strong handshake (confidence), a war hug (love/comfort), a pat on the head (patronizing) or a pat on the back (support/congratulations).
Mirroring	This involves mimicking the other person's gestures, body movement, and even speech patterns, for example, adopting the same sitting posture. Deliberate use of this method can make people feel comfortable in tense situations. Be aware that this can also make the other person feel like you are mocking them, which can erode the benefits.

Use of Space	Don't stand too close and invade another person's personal space. Unless you are trying to be intimate/show affection with them or show aggression/dominance towards them.
Physical Body Changes	These are almost impossible to control consciously and need to be accepted without judgement or excessive concern. For example, people might excessively sweat or blink when they are nervous.

Yep. There are many dimensions to the wonderful world of body language. Lots to think about. Lots to try to overcome. Don't be afraid to try this new secret ingredient and remember to ask your feedback friend to determine how you are doing.

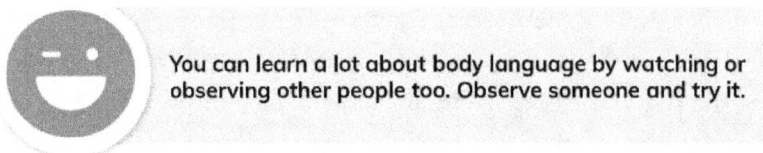

You can learn a lot about body language by watching or observing other people too. Observe someone and try it.

Facial Expression	
Body Movement and Posture	
Gestures	
Eye Contact	
Touch	
Mirroring	
Use of Space	
Physical Body Changes	

The Flavors of Visual Communication

You likely saw some interesting things when you observed people's body language. With practice, you can learn a thing or two about how non-verbal communication contributes to getting your message across.

Undoubtably, you are aware of many different types of communication opportunities where you can't observe someone's body language. These might include virtual meetings, phone calls, emails, and instant messages. And while they might vary in delivery, all these streams typically have one thing in common. Words.

A lot of people think that effective communication is all about words. Here's a little secret: words alone aren't the best way to communicate, if we haven't already convinced you of that. Need proof? Take a pen and paper out and try to describe the shape of Australia using nothing but words. Need another example? Now try to describe what a new color looks like. At this point, you're probably thinking that words might not be the most effective way to communicate these ideas. You would be correct.

In times like these, ultimate praise should go to visual communication! This is the practice of using visual elements to convey a message, inspire change, or evoke emotion.

Visual communication consists of two major parts.

One part is crafting a message that engages the audience and the second part is using graphic design to communicate that message so it's clear and eye-catching. This can be accomplished by pairing your message with visual elements, such as pictures, videos, GIFs, pie charts, slide deck presentations, and infographics. This chapter explores why visual elements are important and how visual communication can be an effective way to get your message across.

The first reason why someone might want to incorporate visual elements to help craft their message is practical. By using them, you save time.

Consider onboarding, for instance. Let's imagine Esther is joining your organization. Since you want Esther to feel welcomed, you decide to schedule a face-to-face training session with her. It's a lot to learn, but you are hopeful she will learn right from the start. What happens instead is that she gets overwhelmed. To overcome this, she asks for another training. You schedule another and then another whenever a new employee like her joins your organization.

In onboarding instances, life can be easier by using a visual element, such as a narrated video. New hires will be able to re-watch them when they have a question. By providing Esther with visual communication, you can avoid time-consuming training sessions.

Besides saving time, another reason visual elements are necessary in your communication is that words can feel downright boring sometimes. When you are trying to get your message across, you can enhance someone's experience by remembering that:

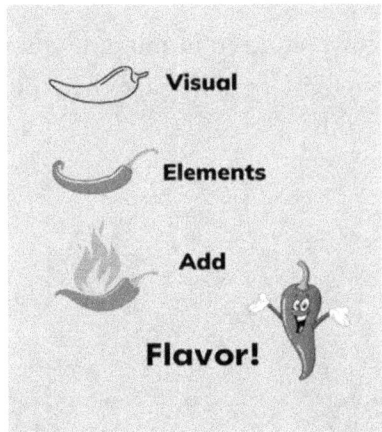

Keep in mind, if you welcome visual communication into your life, while it does add flavor, not everyone will be a good graphic designer. For instance, imagine you had to teach someone named Julian how to design an infographic for a jewelry company called "Forever Stones." In your mind, you might be expecting something like this:

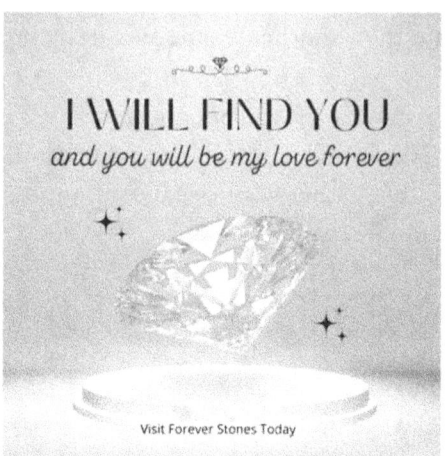

That's not bad. However, keep in mind, if you don't begin by telling Julian what kind of fonts, colors, and shapes he should use, you might end up with something like this:

Eek! That's not the type of attention anyone wants to grab nor is it the flavor you intended. What's worse, is now you must teach Julian how to design a visual element and that will again take time you don't really have.

However, if done right, it's a relief that visual elements can also help you deliver a lot of complex information in a short amount of time. For instance, you might consider giving Julian an infographic that makes graphic design recommendations. We found this one on DesignMantic.com.

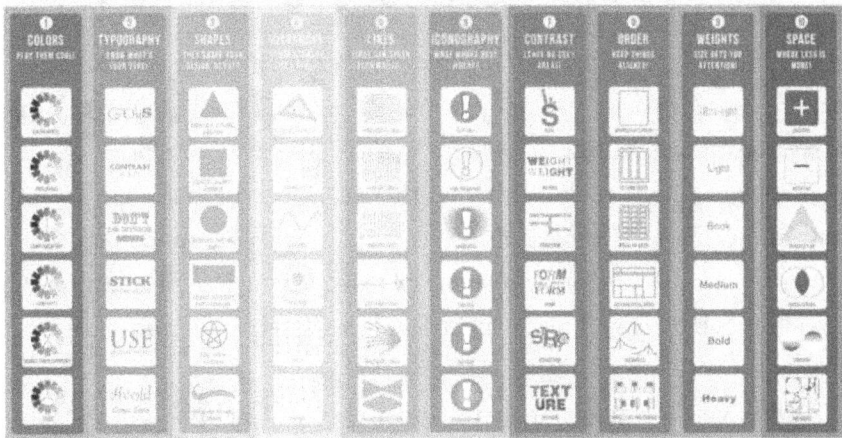

So, visual elements are important since they save time, add flavor, and can help you deliver a lot of information in a short amount of time. But why is visual communication an effective way to get your message across?

Visual communication helps create meaning for your audience. You can use data-driven visual elements to show the impact or intentions of your work. Pictures and icons can be used to make information more memorable. As a result, visual communication can lead to effective and authentic conversation.

Using Questions Effectively

Here's the thing about other people: you can't always tell what they're thinking, even if you are pretty good at reading their body language. Which is why maximizers must also learn how to ask effective questions.

The argument is still out whether there is such a thing as asking a stupid question. As many of us have observed, stupidity lurks around every corner. But since you are obviously a smart person, if you have a question, you should probably ask it. This is called "being a participant in the engagement process."

When you ask questions effectively, they can help you get to know people better. With them, you can learn a lot and you get to participate in interesting conversations.

Questions help you to become more informed about things that matter to you and your success. By asking them, you can extract or collect important information. They can also help you to probe, seek clarification, or gain a better understanding of the things you may need to understand in the future.

Questions ensure people that you are interested in what they are saying, particularly when the topic is important to them. So yes, questions can be used to increase engagement. And a savvy communicator can use them to drive their listeners to participate in insightful thinking.

A well-timed question can spark a fantastic conversation with lots of participation. This sort of engagement takes communication to the next level because your audience will be open and interested in learning more about your message.

When you're reading the room, questioning can help reveal what is unsaid or unknown. Have you ever been in a conversation where you got a sense that the people you were talking to were holding back on saying what they think about you? You might have picked up a bad vibe and suddenly you felt uncomfortable or awkward?

The next time you feel like something isn't quite right, you should go with your gut and address this if you can. Your timing and the way you ask the question will be important, and this approach will reveal unexpected but important information.

Your approach to asking questions should be as a listener, which we will elaborate on in the next chapter. For now, know that the questions listed below, and the different types of question explained later will invite others to share more information. And in return, you will gain the opportunity to fully understand their point of view.

There are four powerful questions that can be used in different situations to help you reveal a person's true thoughts and feelings:

1. Is there a reason we can't...?
2. Can you please explain why you feel this way?
3. Is there any part about what we have discussed that concerns you?
4. What are your thoughts on what I have said?

Once you know someone's true thoughts and feelings, you must learn how to ask them the right types of questions. To unpack how this can be accomplished effectively, let's meet Pete.

Pete was a nice guy who often found himself in situations where he was itching to influence what happened. He just didn't know what to say or do, not realizing that learning to ask the right questions was all he needed.

Pete grew up thinking that the smart people were the ones who always had all the answers. This was the way to *win friends and influence people.*

What Pete didn't know was that it's more impactful to ask a smart question rather than give a smart answer. A great question that is well timed can make a big difference.

One time, Pete found himself in a situation where he felt excluded, like he was being talked at because one or two people were dominating the conversation. He couldn't get a word or thought in.

Then suddenly, someone, who hadn't said anything the whole time, but obviously had been listening and observing, asked a great question. Somehow, the whole tone and direction of the conversation changed. That's when Pete realized the power of a great question!

After researching, planning, and practicing, Pete realized that there were different types of questions that he could use to achieve different outcomes. These questions include open-ended, probing, hypothetical, reflective, deflective, leading, innovating, and closing questions.

Pete decided to use *open-ended questions* out of curiosity, to learn more about something, to uncover facts, and when he needed to gather information. He found this sort of question to be appropriate when starting a conversation or when he was trying to open a new line of thinking for someone.

In one instance, Pete was researching the effects of a heavy workload on people, and he asked, "What do you think about your workload?" As a result, an insightful conversation started.

Pete also realized that he could ask open-ended questions when he was trying to lead someone to a conclusion on their own rather than directly giving them the answer or telling them. All in all, Pete found this method to be a pleasant one and, in the process, learned that he had to make time to listen to people's answers without getting impatient. An open-ended question wasn't appropriate if he needed a quick answer as well.

Probing questions were something that Pete needed more practice with. These are the type of questions that can be used when you only have partial information, when you want to learn a bit more, dig deeper, or gain a better understanding of a topic.

He realized he could use these types of questions after open-ended questions when he wanted to know more about something specific. He could also use them when he felt the other person was rambling on a bit and he wanted to get them back on track.

For example, on his heavy workload assignment, Pete asked a friend, "You mentioned earlier that when your workload is heavy, you feel out of balance. Why is being in balance important to you?"

He also discovered that when he worded his probing questions to seem more like he was curious rather than being too interrogating or judgmental, he learned more about people's feelings, thoughts, and assumptions. In addition, he discovered the facts he needed to gain a better understanding.

Hypothetical questions were Pete's favorite. He loved to use them when he wanted to introduce an idea or suggest a way to do something and get someone else's thoughts. He found this method to be a helpful and less direct way to safely test out the ideas that were still forming in his mind.

For the workload assignment, Pete was preparing to present his ideas on how to manage stress, but he was still unsure of his final position on an issue. He wanted to make sure that when he asked a question, he gave plenty of context on why he was asking it. This way, people would understand what he wanted to know and give him a good response.

After contemplation, he asked the group: "If you were working on too many things at once and feeling stressed and overwhelmed, would you take a break from it all for a day, or power on and hope that it will be okay?"

On a side note, with close friends, Pete often found these types of questions to be rather hilarious when he asked things like, "If you were a pirate who sailed the seas looking for sunken treasure, what would your name be?"

More often with close friends, but sometimes professionally, heavy or controversial topics such as civil rights, affirmative action, vaccinations, etc. came up in conversations. This is where Pete used *reflective questions* to check with people that they were making sense of the topic for themselves.

Pete did this by asking at the right time, usually after a long conversation, "What do you think is clearer for you after that conversation?" He did this in response to anticipating that people might be embarrassed to admit they do not get what he said, so they just went along with it.

Rather than assuming that what he has said is understood, Pete asks reflective questions to measure not only the achievement of his message, but that it was also delivered to a person who is really thinking about what he was saying.

His goal was to not just ask questions such as "Do you understand?" as responses were often one-word answers like "Yes" or "No."

Sometimes situations got awkward for Pete, which is why he is so grateful for *deflective questions*. Pete found it difficult to judge the right timing for these kinds of questions at first, because sometimes people get really heated and emotional about certain topics. To combat irrational thinkers, Pete practiced asking these types of questions whenever possible.

For instance, Pete paid careful attention when participating in a conversation that may have taken a negative direction. He noticed that once people "downloaded" or organized their thoughts, rather than get defensive, an easy way to break the tension was to say, "That's an interesting point. Would it be okay to chat about that later, after I have had more time to think about it?"

Deflective questions helped Pete redirect hostility or resistance. They also helped him avoid destructive conversations because they encouraged unity and cooperation. He found them an effective way to shift the focus of the message to a more positive discussion.

Leading questions were much more fun to ask and often led to accomplishing tasks throughout his day. These are the types of questions Pete used when he wanted to influence the direction of thoughts or actions in others.

He liked that there was a *right* answer to these leading questions (sometimes called loaded questions) that wasn't immediately obvious. The listener, for these types of questions, could be steered to the right answer by how the question was phrased. The question itself contained the information that Pete wanted to confirm.

For example, let's say Pete was meeting his friend Cassandra at the local shopping mall. Pete likes ice cream and Cassandra knows it. He suggests meeting at the ice cream stand and mentions that they both should get an ice cream. When he arrives, he grins and asks his friend, "Do you like ice cream?" And the answer will be definite, *Yes or No*.

Pete also gets those leading questions. They should be avoided if he is trying to discover new and accurate information or insights because leading questions can cover up what people are really thinking, especially if they feel awkward about giving an unpopular or opposing opinion. Being considerate is something Pete is working on. High-five Pete.

Pete deserves another high-five for practicing *innovating questions* too. These are best asked in situations when Pete is trying to brainstorm or when he is feeling open to new ideas.

Let's say he is trying to shape an approach for an assignment, or he has a new product he needs for a customer. His team might get together and gather ideas. He might ask his group, "If money and time are not a constraint for us, what do we want the solution to look like?"

Innovating questions can help you build on your current knowledge, and the knowledge of other people. They are cool because when Pete asks them, he witnesses shifts in perspectives, develops his ideas, has thought provoking moments, and questions opportunities. This sort of question tests his creative thinking and allows Pete to have an open mind to possibilities.

The last type of questions that Pete practices are *closing questions*. These are the type of questions that Pete uses when a discussion feels like it is finished or a decision has been made. He saw a need to ask them because sometimes people are not clear on the next steps or what has been agreed upon.

These questions came in handy after Pete spent a few sessions exploring opportunities and working through options with his peers. Everyone seemed to be on the same page and happy with what had been discussed, but decisions had yet to be made. Pete would inquire of the group, "When will you be able to make a decision about this?" so he could clarify the next steps.

He also found closing questions useful when he felt like a discussion was dragging on and that he was covering old ground. As soon as he realized no new ideas were emerging, he would interject with a closing question to steer the conversation to a close and action.

Patience was a virtue when Pete decided that a conversation was done. He knew that if he used closing questions too early, he could cut short important options that were even better than he had imagined so he resisted this urge.

To summarize, after a person's true thoughts and feeling are revealed, remember to ask them the right type of questions. The right type of questions might include open-ended, probing, hypothetical, reflective, deflective, leading, innovating, and closing questions.

Type	When to Ask
Open-ended	Ask when you want to learn more about something, out of curiosity, to uncover facts, and when you need to gather information.
Probing	Ask when you only have partial information, when you want to learn a bit more, dig deeper, or gain a better understanding of a topic.
Hypothetical	Ask when you want to introduce an idea or suggest a way to do something and get someone else's thoughts.
Reflective	Ask when you want to check in with people that they are making sense of the topic for themselves.
Deflective	Ask when you want to redirect hostility, resistance, or destructive conversations.
Leading	Ask when you want to influence the direction of thoughts or actions in others.
Innovating	Ask when you are feeling open to new ideas and when you are trying to brainstorm.
Closing	Ask when you feel like the discussion is finished or a decision has been made.

Maximizers and Pete know that asking the right question at the right time can change things dramatically, hopefully, for the better. They try to plan and practice their responses so that their discussions have solutions.

Impactful communicators, who want success, have a lot to think about and juggle: what they say, how they say it, and trying to effectively ask questions at the same time. Yikes. Sounds tricky but it is possible! The secret is recognizing how to listen.

Be an Active Listener

Remember that childhood story about the hare and the tortoise? The recap: the hare was in a hurry to win the race, got too confident, took a nap, and then the tortoise won.

After many years in the corporate world and after having many conversations with professionals, we have learned that life is kind of like this story. A lot of people are in a hurry to become excellent communicators, but the truth is, they first need to learn to become a good listener. Being a good communicator is knowing when it's time to slow down like the tortoise and listen versus when it's time to hurry up and talk like the hare. It's means paying attention to verbal as well as non-verbal messages. And it's working on your holistic delivery approach (what to say and how to say it) all together.

With this is mind, be unapologetically truthful now, *How good are you at listening?* Not pretending to listen, really listening. Listening with the intention to understand.

Not sure? Let's see. Ask yourself these two questions:

1. Do you always remember the names of the people you are introduced to while you are still in a conversation with them?

2. Can you always recall something someone has said that gives you a clue into who they are or what's important to them?

If you said, "No," to either question, you probably have already accepted the fact that listening is sometimes hard to do. *But why?*

Research indicates that 25% of people listen effectively.[xxxiii] This number is so low because our lives are full of distractions. Smartphones. Studying. Working. That program. Those shiny things. Daily life in general. These distractions have conditioned many of us to have a short attention span. We lack the focus to listen intently for unified success.

Then there is that other mixed bag. Most of us believe we're listening, but often we are just pretending to listen while we are thinking about how to respond. Most people think about what they want to say in reply or what advice they want to give when it's their turn to talk. Instead, more people should listen to understand. This is called *active listening*.

Active listening or real listening is an essential human skill that is often lacking. Most people don't know how to give someone their full attention. When you listen, you should try to absorb all the relevant information provided to you through non-verbal and verbal cues.

Even if you think you are good at it, half-listening, or not-listening at all can be obvious to others. A person should listen actively if they want to build relationships and trust.

Active listening is a good idea since it helps you not only better understand but also retain information. This way, when you respond, you don't look like an idiot. Instead, you have based your decisions or responses on more complete or correct information.

Maximizers demonstrate active listening in a bunch of ways. One way is by using their non-verbal cues to show that they're indeed listening.

You can achieve this by doing things like nodding or making eye contact with the people you are with. This method lets them know you are carefully considering their words and even enjoying what they are trying to say.

Do this and always remember as Mike Irving, peak performance facilitator, proclaims, "If no one listens, it doesn't matter how much talking happens, there is no communication."[xxxiv]

Another way maximizers demonstrate active listening is by mentally preparing for the possibility of disruptions. These can occur when you are trying to actively listen, so you need to prepare for them ahead of time. To practice, you can think about what you will do if disruptions occur. This will make the difference between communicating your message successfully versus failing to deliver it.

If disruptions happen, you can maximize your potential by remembering to **SMILE**. This is an especially helpful method to use in a classroom setting with students who are insistent on disrupting you:

S.M.I.L.E.

Smile warmly.

Make eye contact.

Initiate your response by thanking the listener for the question or comment then responding the best you can. (Thanking disruptive people typically throws them off).

Listen to the response and ask if you addressed the concern.

Energize your communication to be confident, encouraging the disruptive person to back down.

If someone is asking a difficult question or provoking you for a reaction, it's important to remember that difficult questions can be tricky. Give yourself a break sometimes. After all, practicing and navigating disruptions when you are trying to be an active listener is something that not only Pete, but everyone needs to work on.

Alas, even in your best active listening moments, not all communication goes as expected and sometimes people get emotional. In the next chapter you'll see what we mean by meeting our next human-example, Jane.

Don't Let Your Worries Consume You

Jane sometimes gets worried. She describes it as feeling debilitating because she fears being put on the spot and not knowing what to say. For this reason, Jane is terrified whenever she must go on an interview. This is especially true if she really wants the job.

For years, Jane had to work on keeping her cool when she got thrown a curveball or an impromptu question that was difficult to answer. Even in the best of times, she found connecting with people challenging and stressful.

If she didn't have time to prepare, it was harder. She had moments when she thought about saying something that made her look bad. Sometimes *gulp* she even said inappropriate things to other people.

Public speaking and unexpected questions made her nauseous and her discomfort level increased to the extreme. What she needed was to develop the skills and techniques to help her conquer her anxiety and shine regardless of the challenges.

First things first. Jane can't panic or freeze, and she should avoid jumping on top of the conference table while screaming, "I don't know! I don't know!" in front of her colleagues.

Jokes aside, unexpected things happen all the time and this can be particularly scary when you are new to a job or trying to prove yourself to new people. In those times, maximizers assure people like Jane that they can follow a few tips to take on the challenge.

If want to help someone like Jane, you can remind her to take a deep breath to help settle her nerves. Assure her with, "You are capable of doing this." And recommend she try the **WAKE** method:

What's the worst that can happen?
Assume that the person has genuinely asked you the question because they want to hear what you think. Be assured they are not trying to trick you or make you look bad. They don't have some weird gamma ray that will dissolve all your clothing, forcing you to have this conversation in your

underwear. If the worst thing to happen is that you're wrong or look a little foolish, the world isn't going to end.

Ask for a moment or two to collect your thoughts.

Don't be afraid to ask for a few moments to gather your thoughts. When a person asks an unexpected question, they should not expect an instant and polished answer! This tip is especially useful in interviews. Just politely ask for a few seconds and give yourself the gift of thinking about what you are going to say.

If you didn't hear the question properly or are not sure if you understood it, you should ask the person to say the question again. But this time, really listen to what they are saying to make sure you are clear. We don't recommend asking for a third time. Take it from us. It's not a good look.

Keep it short and simple. (KISS, or sometimes humorously referred to as keep it simple, stupid.)

Keep the response short and simple and do not ramble. We know this isn't easy when you're nervous, under pressure, or have no idea what you want to say. We are going to go over how to respond to questions shortly, so if this concerns you, keep your hat on and read that section later.

Energy and body language will help you "fake it until you make it."

Try to give your response as much positive energy as you can despite the nerves. Watch that you don't give it TOO much energy, as you may seem obviously flustered. Remember that the non-verbal (your voice, tone, body language etc.) is even more important than what you say.

Jane is starting to get the idea now, but she is thinking, "What the hell should I say if I have no idea what to say?" We would tell her to use the WAKE method as a clever way to buy herself more thinking time even if she did understand the question the first time. Either way, when she is listening to the question being repeated, she can steady her nerves by breathing slowly.

We would also tell her to thank the person for their question and to maintain good eye contact with the speaker. Apart from being polite, softening her face, smiling, and showing she is relaxed is a good idea.

Finally, we would tell Jane not to spend all her time thinking about what to say. There's a lot to think about in the few moments between being asked an unexpected question and answering it. She should resist the urge to just think about *what* she is going to say and instead focus on *how* you are going to say it, which is just as important.

"So, if I get an unexpected question, *how* am I going to respond?" Jane panicky asks. We would tell Jane that having some well-practiced techniques to use when the unexpected questions get asked is highly recommended.

Response Techniques for Questions

Sometimes you are having a public or private conversation and you think things are going smoothly. This is a great feeling. But, sigh, it doesn't always last. Someone will inevitably ask you a question you don't know how to answer, and then you will need some time to recover your thoughts. Sometimes you knew they would ask it, and other times you are shocked by the fact that they posed such a question. Either way, in these moments, you should use response techniques so you can get back to business sooner.

It should be noted that in certain instances, one technique will clearly fit best, while at other times, you may have to combine a few. Regardless, there are four response techniques for expected, unexpected, or difficult questions.

The first technique is **PREP or point, reason, example, point.** Use this technique when you want to convince someone, and you have a great personal example to back it up.

Make a simple **point** that addresses the subject of the question.

Provide a good **reason** for making that point and why it's valid or important.

Provide a relevant, personal **example** that reinforces your point of reasoning.

Come back to your **point** to conclude the actions/steps that you took, what your results were, or what you learned.

For example, if the question to Jane was, "Why do you think impromptu speaking is a great skill to have?" She would say:

Point - "Impromptu speaking is a real skill."

Reason - "It's important to always be ready for unexpected situations."

Example - "This happened to me recently in a group learning session when I was asked about a topic that I didn't know a lot about."

Point - "I paused and forced myself to see this as an opportunity. Even though I got the answer wrong, I learned something when the right answer was given."

The second technique is called **past, present, future.** You can also use this response technique when you want to *convince* someone, but you really can't think of a great personal example.

Start by describing what your previous situation (**past**).

What your situation is now (**present**).

And what you expect to happen next (**future**).

So, if Jane was asked, "What will you gain if you continue developing your impromptu speaking skills?" She would say:

Past - "When I was put on the spot in the past, I worried about looking foolish. Regardless, I did my best to answer."

Present - "As a result of taking this approach, I know the world doesn't end when I don't have an answer. I know I must remain confident and keep practicing this important skill."

Future - "In the future, if I stick with this mindset and stay open to improving, I know I can be ready for any situation."

The third response technique is all about *why* something happened and what you did about it. It's called the **cause, effect, remedy** technique, and it's used when behavior-based questions are asked.

Start with describing the problem (the context) and the **cause** of the current issue.

Describe what is currently happening as an **effect** or because of that problem.

Outline what needs to be done or actions you need to take to **remedy** the cause of the problem.

Jane might be asked, "How do you think people can overcome a fear of speaking or being put on the spot?" She could respond with:

Cause - "A fear of public speaking, especially when put on the spot with an unexpected question, can really hold you back."

Effect - "The effect of giving into this fear means you are unlikely to ever develop and improve this important life skill."

Remedy - "Thinking that every opportunity is a learning opportunity will help you overcome your fear of being wrong or looking like a fool."

A last technique can be used when Jane has to explain *how* something happened in the first place. It's simply called **before**, the **event**, the **result**.

Describe what the situation was **before** an event (or series of events) occurred.

Describe the **event** that happened to bring about a change to that situation.

Describe the impact of that change as a **result** of the event.

Jane should know exactly what to say when someone asks her, "How did you overcome a fear of public speaking or being put on the spot?" She would reflectively vocalize:

Before - "I used to hate answering questions on the spot."

The Event - "Then I got a great job in management and one of the requirements of the position was to participate in team meetings."

Result - "I decided to make a concerted effort to remain calm and play to my strengths when answering an unexpected question in the meetings. It took me a little while to get there, and lots of practice, but I'm no longer afraid of looking a little foolish in front of my team. Sometimes I even enjoy answering questions that are not easy. I feel a sense of pride and accomplishment when it's done."

Even when Jane becomes familiar with these four techniques, she must practice them regularly. She will continue to have moments where she just goes blank and lets her nerves get the best of her. But with practice, these moments will become fewer and fewer.

It can be tricky to conquer your worries of being asked unexpected questions. Again, it's okay. When this happens, be honest with yourself and remember that we are all human. No one has all the answers. Especially when we are trying to navigate difficult situations, such as dealing with a conflict or delivering bad news.

No one likes being asked unexpected questions, but they're unavoidable. It helps to have response techniques in your toolkit, so you know how to approach them when they do occasionally happen.

You can Make a Positive Impact

Maximizing your potential means effectively communicating in every situation so you can get more out of yourself and others. It means doing more in less time and achieving better results that make a positive impact.

Some people think that avoiding negative interactions, such as difficult conversations or questions, is a way to positively make an impact. This is not the case. At some point, you will have the experience of delivering unwanted news or be in a conflict with someone.

You will also have uncomfortable experiences. No one wants to be the person who is put on the spot and then says something that made someone feel bad, upset, or even deeply hurt. And yes, there is always a possibility that your response will put people off or damage relationships. But avoiding these negative situations only brings you temporary relief.

The way to begin effectively communicating is to not let any issues become bigger than they need to be. Whenever you feel a conflict building up, do yourself a favor, and try to address it sooner rather than later. Ignoring it, hoping it goes away, will rarely work out for you.

Before you do anything else, try to take a rational approach by acknowledging that the situation is impacting everyone, not just you. Think through how everyone might feel and why things are happening as they are.

If you want to make a positive impact, try to be the kind of person you like dealing with, a person who is understanding, one who suspends their own anger, disappointment, frustration, and fear. Your thought process should be that you want to work this out and move forward.

Waiting for someone else to step in and make life better is not a good plan. Reality is there's no one better than you to step in and try to change things when there is a difficult situation. Do not delay things unnecessarily and know that you can make a positive impact. *How?*

You can lead by example. If the conversation becomes difficult, remember it doesn't matter whose fault it is. What matters is moving beyond what is holding everyone, including you, from moving forward. Instead, acknowledge your barriers and communication types, then address them accordingly.

You can be careful on how you phrase what you say so that you can avoid defensiveness. For instance, think about *how* you deliver a difficult message. When people feel like it's okay to be wrong, there is a far greater chance they will bring their authentic self to the relationship. Maximizers recognize the importance, formality, and circumstances of a conversation.

As you practice these things we've discussed, combine it with the unity you're also trying to achieve in groups. When communicating in a group setting, you can make sure people know that you care about them. To do this, be curious about who they are, get to know them on a deeper level, and be your genuine self. When people sense you are being honest, they are more likely to trust you and let their guard down. As a result, they will flourish, and you will feel great about it.

In a group setting, you should make sure all participants in the conversation review the options for any alternative solutions. If there is time for discussion, people can make a choice on the best solution. For this, use some sort of voting approach. In a classroom, sometimes popsicle sticks with names can be drawn, so time is not wasted on inconsequential decisions such as who will read the next passage.

But either way, be inclusive when making decisions. Don't leave people out of making a choice that can affect the group. People don't like working with other people who try to control everything and prefer to have a say on things that impact them rather than being told what to do.

You can commit to sticking to the chosen solution. Try to have some fun with this one. If you pick sticks, for example, shake them around in a (The Hunger Games themed) jar and proudly exclaim, "May the odds be ever in your favor."

You can know the value of planning and crafting your message. Do this with the knowledge of a few effective communication ground rules or understandings for the people participating in the conversation. For example, *the group will...*

Collaborate and approach decisions or conflicts with intentions of resolving the problem.

Have a willingness to listen to everyone in the group.

Have the courage to express their opinions even when it is unpopular.

Suspend judgement of others and proceed into discussions with an open mind.

Collectively work towards a positive outcome.

You can follow the effective communication *Dos and Don'ts*. They will help you to maximize your potential and the potential of others.

Do *these things:*

Take the first step and ask questions to understand the other person's point of view. *Actively listen* to what they say. Recap what has been said to demonstrate you get it. This shows your understanding of others.

Use positive body language to project confidence and positivity, even when you don't want to, and make eye contact.

Use words that show you want to do what it takes to resolve the issue and move forward. In most cases, other people will follow your lead.

Try and find one thing that all parties can agree on. Let go of your need to be right. This will loosen things up and open the door to the possibility of resolution.

Remain calm. It'll help the other parties feel safe rather than threatened.

Keep an open mind to other perspectives. You may start seeing things differently.

Treat others the way you expect to be treated.

Include yourself in statements about your opinions and decisions, for example, "I think that's a great idea" versus, "That's a great idea." They both mean the same, but the first statement is far more personal.

Don't *do these things:*

See others as opponents or the enemy.

Stay quiet and hold back from sharing your opinion, even if it's unpopular.

Use threatening language and raise your voice to show dominance.

Dig your heels in to get your way at all costs.

Disregard what is being said even though you may not agree.

Lastly, you can make a positive impact by evaluating yourself and practicing your skills such as: knowing your barriers, crafting your message, effective storytelling, feedback, listening, adaptation, conquering your anxiety, and responding to questions. Then you can effectively communicate what you have learned with other people.

Part Four

"A"

<u>Advocate</u> For Practicing Human Skills

"You win conclusively when you turn your opponent into a believer and supporter of your case."
— **Arne Næss**[xxxv]

ADVOCATE

Imagine we told you that it would be beneficial to dedicate yourself to charity for a month's time. You might be thinking, "Well I know that's nice and all, but I'm not sure I'm interested in doing that." That's because you have all the capability to dedicate yourself to something, just not the correct incentive. But what if we said that we would give you one hundred thousand dollars to dedicate yourself? We bet you would certainly be willing to try now.

We thought a lot about incentive as we tried to make sense of what it really means to dedicate yourself as an advocate of human skills. If not money, what would drive you to actively be "a person who pleads another's cause, or who speaks or writes in support of something"?[xxxvi]

This is especially difficult to answer since it is common knowledge that good advocates need the kind of dedication is rarely appreciated by others. In fact, many advocates volunteer their time or are compensated very little for work that they do.

Just the same, there is certainly evidence of well compensated advocates. A CEO, for example, is an advocate when she demonstrates excellence through representation of her company in person and on social media. A social worker will advocate for his clients by helping them access services such as housing, food, utilities, and medical service. In education, advocates work with governments, universities, communities, districts, families, staff, and students, just to name a few.

So, what's the appeal for you becoming an advocate yourself? The appeal is you can increase people's awareness of how to initiate change for a better world -- in your case, by imparting knowledge of the traits people need to function in a thriving society.

This section in about the human skills needed to ensure that people's voices are heard on issues that are important to them. When you master these human skills yourself, you can then advocate them in others. Only then can you protect and promote the rights of others by acting with focused intention.

Eventually, you can become an effective advocate who knows how to leverage your strengths. And, when it's an appropriate time, you will be able to remind your team of the goals they are trying to accomplish.

You might ask, "How?" Start by believing. Say an advocate's words aloud to yourself every day:

I am honest and I am not afraid to ask difficult questions.
I demonstrate unity by encouraging others to recognize their potential.
I am a maximizer who helps people accomplish their goals.
I am a leader and an advocate of human skills.
People like me change the world for the better.

Time for an Activity!

In addition to repeating an advocate's words daily, you can learn to become an advocate by being aware of all those who have advocated for you. In gratitude, make a "Thanks for being an Advocate" post on your favorite social media to demonstrate how much you appreciate the dedication the person has shown to his or her cause.

Don't forget to tag the person and include #successishuman

Recognize Mindfulness and Balance

Mindfulness involves being in the moment mentally as well as physically. Some people think it's just a word that describes a lot of hippy-dippy bullshit. If you think that you need to check your horoscope now before we proceed, rest easy.

We can assure you that no matter what you have heard about the topic, there are some legit points that can be made about mindfulness, and we know that advocates who are successful people practice the skills involved regularly.

If you are going to be an advocate, you will need to develop mindfulness skills. Learning this skill allows you to advocate for it or impart this knowledge to others. Mindful people know what it means to live in the moment and have a sense of presence in everything they do. Mindfulness enables them to focus on their current experience by fully bringing their attention to what is going on at the time. They don't dwell on the past. They don't worry too much about the future.

Without mindfulness, an advocate's brain will feel like it is in a constant competition with priorities, being attacked by your to-do list and running in different directions at the same time. This feeling can make you anxious, stressed, and overwhelmed.

Let's play a mindfulness game of how to recognize if you are struggling with mindfulness as a skill. Ask yourself the following questions:

> Do you ever feel like your brain is a computer and you have a million tabs open?

> Are you easily prone to distraction when you try to focus on one thing?

> Do you ever feel feel spread too thin and that you are half doing things?

> Do you ever feel guilty, like you're not achieving and completing things the way you want?

> Do you ever feel like you're constantly trying to stop the snowball of negative feelings from taking over your life?

If you answered YES to any of these questions, being aware of how mindfulness will help you become an advocate is information you need to hear.

Being present can help you as an advocate feel calm and confident in the choices you make. A regular practice of mindfulness makes it possible for you to appropriately control your frustration and anger when your needs are not met.

We can show you how practicing mindfulness can play out in a normal situation by introducing you to our friend, Spencer. Spencer wants to be a successful advocate, but he gets angry easily.

One day he was in a rush and went to the grocery store to grab dinner. While shopping, he encountered a few things that only contributed to his anger. An inconsiderate lady blocked his aisle as she lingered over a can of corn, the store was out of his favorite cereal, and to top it all off, clerks were unavailable.

Spencer wanted to discuss the fact that the milk he wanted was not stocked, and now he had to lean his head into the freezer for his inquiry. As Spencer forcibly grabbed the handle of the freezer, he realized (by paying attention to his body language) that his frustration and anger were being triggered by his need to get the groceries quickly.

He recognized that this unmet need might affect the conversation. He decided to have empathy by using an impulse control skill. This involved Spencer deferring the conversation about the milk to a later time when he felt more relaxed.

Spencer breathed deeply as he shopped for the next item on his list. When feeling calmed, he recognized that he needed to be less defensive and more patient. The clerk was very busy, overwhelmed by the insufficient inventory, and wasn't trying to be difficult.

You know what Spencer learned that day? That mindfulness can decrease stress and relieve the pressures of the day. This same knowledge can be applied to his workplace and in his home.

Advocates understand that excessive stress and pressure are factors at odds with a balanced life. When they are in touch with what triggers them and their emotions, this enables them to be more in touch with the emotions of others. The calm and focus from mindfulness help Spencer feel more in control and better equipped to make good decisions.

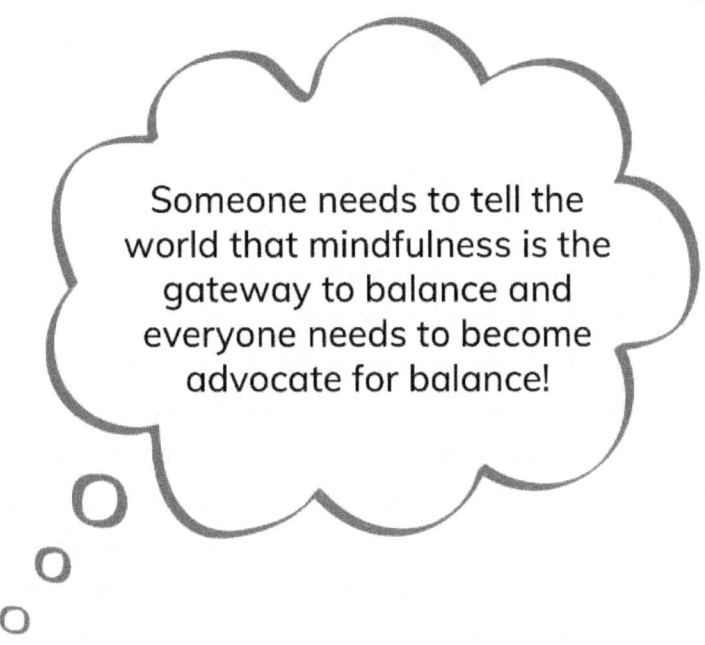

Someone needs to tell the world that mindfulness is the gateway to balance and everyone needs to become advocate for balance!

It helps him find perspective, build resilience, and have the confidence to cope with challenges. Through all these benefits, mindfulness helps Spencer find the right balance between everything that is going on in his life. He is excited to advocate for this skill for those around him.

No one understood this better than Mr. Miyagi from the famous Karate Kid movies.[xxxvii] He explained to his student Daniels, "Balance is key." Balance is essential in our lives so we, like Daniel, can do things we want and need to do without over or under investing in certain parts of our lives. Mindfulness helps advocates get there by giving them the clarity to make good decisions about where they should invest their time.

Whether it's learning karate, in the grocery store, spending time with their significant other, in the workplace, or something else altogether, balance is how advocates invest their life in a way that satisfies their needs. This enables them to do their best and share this skill with others.

An advocate's life is made up of many vital areas including their health, family, finances, studies, social, work, spirituality, recreation, personal growth, romance, the list goes on and on. They won't always spend time every day in each area in equal amounts, but if in the long run, they spend a sufficient quantity and quality of time in each area, their life will feel in balance.

When balance is achieved, advocates feel whole and complete because they don't feel like they are neglecting any part of their lives. Finding balance is an essential life skill that if not practiced, can lead to people or relationships suffering. We are advocates of mindfulness because we believe that if people are not careful about how they prioritize the things in their lives, they will find themselves without balance, become overwhelmed, and invest in things that don't align with their values or needs.

Save the nervous nail-biting for someone who has time for it. Finding balance needs to happen now and it is a realistic goal that is easy to achieve. Advocates consciously align their choices to their values and needs.

For many people, the practice of proactively creating balance is a foreign concept but learning how to develop this skill will help them get through the stress of life with a sense of sanity. There will be times when their personal/social life or study/work life will collide. This stinks and sometimes it requires sacrifices.

Balance is possible. Trust the case studies. For example, as one of the most prominent advocates for work-life balance, Arianna Huffington[xxxviii] has spent over a decade fine-tuning and refining her routine to get the most of her day while maintaining balance in her life.

This realization came to her in April of 2007, when the Huffington Post co-founder woke up in a pool of her own blood after collapsing from sleep deprivation and exhaustion. It was from that point on that she made a drastic change to her lifestyle. She said, "For me, that day literally changed my life. It put me on a course in which I changed how I work and how I live," and this led to the launch of her advocacy work at Thrive Global.[xxxix] This drastic change was made with the realization that people need to prioritize themselves.

Again, the term mindfulness gets blanketed into statements like your inner life and outer life will be in harmony, but the truth is, people will never be fulfilled in life if they are not balanced. This needs to be recognized.

Embracing mindfulness allows you to be an advocate for people who want to get back on track when their life is feeling out of balance. In the next chapter we will explore tips on how you can begin your advocate journey by finding and maintaining the human skill of balance even when life gets tricky.

Balance is a Quest

Ever meet someone who broke up with their significant other and they didn't see the signs that their partner was unhappy? While we are not able to help repair that relationship, we can hook you up with the knowledge of signs your life may be out of balance.

You cannot be an advocate of balance for yourself or others if your to-do list is multiple pages long or you can't capture everything you need to do. You might say things like, "I have so much to do and no time to do it." Likewise, you might feel you are constantly busy, but you are not sure you're accomplishing anything at all.

You are also not being an advocate of balance if you feel constantly tired and easily irritated. This can lead to feelings like you are living someone else's schedule and have lost your direction and control. The same is true when you have feelings as though you're moving through life with no choices, no purpose, or the freedom to pursue your priorities.

This includes difficulties like you can't concentrate, make decisions, or feel confident in your abilities and handling problems. If that isn't enough, let's add crappy stuff like lacking motivation, energy, and patience. You didn't forget about your feeling burned out and physical health problems, did you? That too.

If any of these signs seem all too relatable to you, you might be experiencing the deep effects of having an imbalanced life. That makes life challenging enough, but if you are trying to be an advocate to those around you, this imbalance will throw off any advocacy you are attempting.

The point is, all these are signs that your relationships may be headed for trouble because your ability to communicate effectively is undoubtably affected. This may also be a sign that your performance at work or in school is about to decline. Beware.

Light is at the end of the unbalanced tunnel. It can be seen when advocates, like you, look at the whole picture. Take our buddy Abe for example.

Abe wants to have a balanced life, so he decides to analyze all the important areas in his life that need his attention. Abe thinks about each category and rates his satisfaction level on a 0 - 10 scale. In this case, 0 is not satisfied at all and 10 is extremely satisfied. Here are Abe's results:

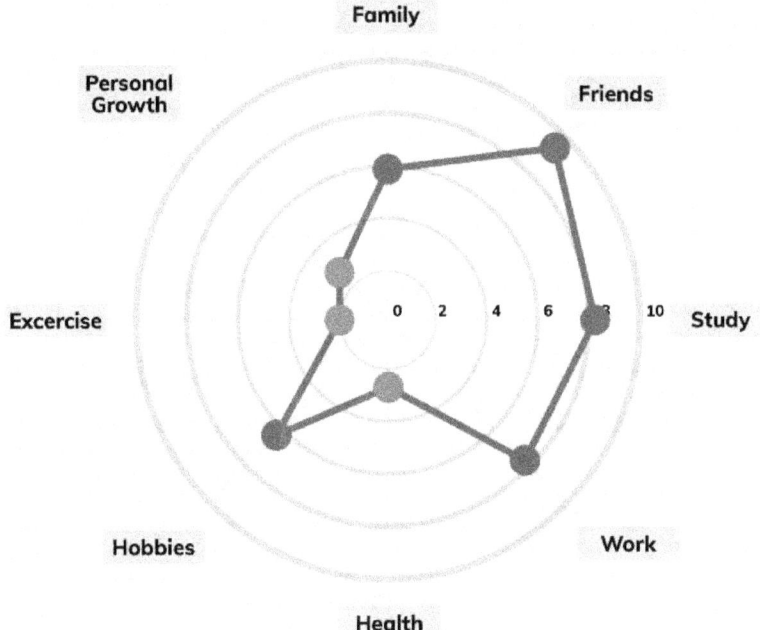

Focusing on the three red dots are Abe's ticket to having a balanced life. They are the areas where the lowest levels of satisfaction exist for him. To become a better advocate for this human skill, Abe must change his perspective to address the deficiencies in his own self-care areas. He must shift his mindset to acknowledge the importance of his personal growth, health, and wellness.

For now, Abe must make choices to prioritize those things. The key to achieving balance will be for Abe to eventually focus on all areas of his life, reaching a level that he is satisfied with.

Finding balance is a continuous process on the path of being a human skills advocate. As you grow, you'll find more ways to integrate the different aspects of your life into a whole. Whether it's yourself, your partner, your children, or your career, no doubt your priorities will change overtime.

We'd love to tell you how much time it will take for you to achieve it, but it's kind of impossible to say because balance is on an individual case-by-case basis. The right balance for you might look very different from someone else's version of balance. Some people need a lot of downtime to relax, while others like to be busy much of the time. Some people like being more connected and social, while others appreciate more time on their own.

Some think it's a priority to prepare for their annual under-water basket weaving contest and some people are preparing for a vacation that involves an Elvis impersonation show. The point is, we all have different needs and wants, so don't get caught up striving for someone else's version of balance. Your balance can be found only by understanding what does and doesn't work for you. Give it a try yourself.

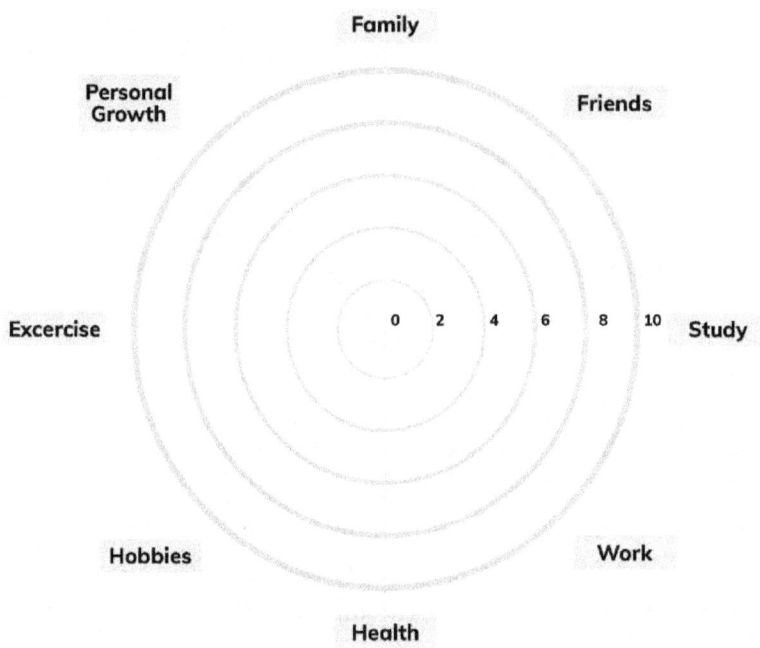

Even though your version of balance is unique, in general, we have **a few tips that can help you become an advocate for yourself and others to find and maintain balance in life.**

Pro Tip #1: Acknowledge and accept that you cannot do everything. We understand the desire to accomplish a lot and please everyone, but this is a never-going-to-happen situation. *Why?* Because you only have so much time, energy, money, and capabilities to give. You are one person and managing everything is impossible.

Be realistic about your intentions. Stop and take a deep breath and welcome to the shit show of all the crap that needs to get done. Regroup and admit that all you can do is all you can do. And it's going to be okay.

Pro Tip #2: Manage your choices. Some days, you may wish you had more time to finish an assignment, study for an exam, hang out with friends, run errands, or get more rest. Whatever the situation, another hard truth is that you unfortunately cannot create more time. We all have the exact same amount each day. But you can, on most days, choose what you do with the time you have.

Managing yourself means making deliberate choices. It reflects a sense of responsibility in what you do in a day and what you can accomplish in a lifetime. When you realize your power to choose, you become a proactive person who knows what they can control.

Your choices should become routine. Be intentional in what you put on your calendar. Choose to make yourself a priority and schedule some time for you to do what gives you comfort, health, joy, or whatever you most need at the time. This includes making the time to eat a balanced diet, exercise, and get plenty of sleep. Become your own best friend in this way and you will be able to accomplish more.

Choosing to make yourself a priority involves asking yourself, "What am I you willing to give up in order to have or achieve something more important?" You need to be prepared to cut back on some activities from your schedule, even if it is just temporary, so you can accomplish higher priorities.

Naturally, there are things that you really must do, like pay bills, schoolwork, sleep, your job, or take care of your health. It's the moments in between the things you must do that need this attention. When planning your week, determine which tasks or activities are less important and can wait. Remove these from the week's to-do list, and you will automatically feel a sense of relief.

The same applies to the people in your life, since the company you keep is often a choice. Spend and make time for the most important people in your life. These are the ones who support you and make you happy. Where possible, sacrifice the amount of time you spend with people who drain you. When you have less stress, you will feel more energized, and this will fuel you to be more productive.

Don't be afraid to make the choice of saying "No." Some people love asking for favors and their approaches to obtaining them may vary. They might say things like: "Will you…? I just need a small favor…, We can always count on you. You're so good at…" When you hear these messages, you might feel flattered, annoyed, or used. Regardless, you should always be asking yourself, "What will happen if I say no?"

Sometimes people choose to say, "Yes," to things because they feel pressured to give an immediate answer or they feel obligated to please the person who is asking them for a favor. In any case, remember that you have the right to think about what you can reasonably do before responding.

Check in with yourself to ask whether doing what is being asked of you aligns with your values. You can choose to say, "No," if you don't want to do something. It's also okay for others to choose to say, "No," to you.

Know when it's time to make a choice. At some point in time, you will feel overwhelmed. Recognize the situation and look at where and how you spend your time. Then cut back on certain things.

Ask yourself questions like, "Am I involved in too many extracurricular activities or organizations? Would this be a good time to drop a leadership role? Should I really be taking all these classes? Do I have to drop attending that video game convention?" Whatever the case, to omit things that eat up a lot of time is not a sign of failure. It's more like the first step towards achieving the balancing act.

When you can, choose to find the funny side. Try to see the amusing side of things especially when things get hard. This may sound weird as an approach to serious things, but the reality is most things are never as bad as they seem. Even with the most terrible of situations, laughter helps lift how bad you are feeling and increases your energy levels.

Ever heard of the saying, "Laughter is the best medicine"? A famous American doctor Patch Adams would strap on a red nose and walk the wards of terminal patients to make them laugh. In return, they would forget their pain and suffering even if only for a short time.[xl]

This may seem strange and forced for some people, but you will see the difference humor can make on your positive mindset. Science supports that laughing is good for you - It leads to the body releasing happy hormones.[xli] So go with it, because bad things will happen, and laughter can be a far more positive and powerful response to life's challenges. Finding humor is a choice.

Pro Tip #3: Own the things you can control. Later in this advocate section, we will go more in depth about "Owning It." For now, you should know that this is something people have been talking about for centuries. Stoic philosopher of first-century Rome, Epictetus, suggested the importance of knowing what we can control and what we can't. His general prescription for a balanced life was simply this: Control what you can and let go of what you can't control.[xlii]

The most basic lesson here is that you should spend the maximum amount of your time on things that can be influenced by your actions. You must also heavily reduce or eliminate the things you are concerned about but cannot control. You can increase either the list of things that concern you or the list of things you can influence.

For example, you can choose to spend your time being concerned about the weather, sickness, the fact that your birthday falls on a Monday, anything. Stress can consume you like an unforgiving tidal wave if you allow it, OR you can choose to spend your time focusing on things you can influence, like your success or your sustainable and healthy relationships that are built by action, not emotion or drama. Focus on the things that are within your control because they will directly impact the kind of balanced life you want to live.

Advocates of balance share the above three tips by offering them to people they care about and applying them in their own lives. As Dr. Robyn L. Gobin, psychologist and educator notes, "Self-care is, fundamentally, about bringing balance back into a life that has grown imbalanced from too many commitments or responsibilities."[xliii]

This advice can be helpful in stressful situations that will inevitably happen as part of life. In those instances, you should remind yourself of the pro tips that can help you reach your goal of sustaining balance over time.

Finding balance is not a comfortable process. While the outcome is often freeing and empowering, the process requires us to push, challenge, and stretch the boundaries of our comfort zones. This can be especially important to accept when unexpected obligations come up and you must re-evaluate your priorities. You can feel balanced one day and unbalanced the next. The idea is for most days to be on track.

How do you know when you are coming close to tasting the magic balanced sauce? By feeling content with your responses to the two following questions:

> When I've taken care of everything I need to do, do I have time and energy to enjoy the things I want to do?

> Can I get absorbed in something without worrying about another task or feeling guilty because I am not doing something else?

Being an advocate of human skills means you know that mindfulness is something that all people should care about. Balance is a part of that knowledge as is resilience or the ability to recover quickly when things get difficult. Yes, being an advocate can be a difficult journey. In the next chapter, we will explore the seas of resilience.

Resilience is Your Lifeboat

Physiologically speaking, *stress* is your body's response to difficult changes that create the challenging demands in your life. We think it's a real shame that in our society it has such a negative connotation.

Not all stress is created equal, and we think more people should stick up for stress's reputation. There is a big difference between good stress, known as eustress, and bad stress, known as distress. We are here to set the record straight.

If you're under *eustress*, it will typically be a motivating experience for you. This kind of stress helps you focus your energy on a specific task. This feeling usually lasts for a short time, and it can feel exciting and improve your performance!

You might be aware of eustress in different activities such as when you are playing a sport or performing for an audience. Its aliases are euphoria, momentum, adrenaline, etc. It should be noted that an event that may be the cause of this positive stress for you may be a negative stress for someone else - everyone reacts to stress differently. Some examples include starting a new job, being promoted, having a baby, getting married, moving to a new house, riding a rollercoaster, going on a holiday, and many more.

Negative stress or *distress* looks and feels very different to eustress. It can cause anxiety and/or concern. It could last for a short time or over the long term. It is perceived to be outside a person's ability to cope. It doesn't feel pleasant, will decrease your performance, and could lead to mental or physical health problems. No bueno.

Some sources of negative stress include death of a close friend or family member, financial problems, the end of a relationship, losing your job, sickness or injury, excessive workload, conflicts at work, etc.

Again, remember that we all respond to stress differently. So, what you experience as negative stress may not be the same as someone else. Either way, everyone should avoid the stress spiral where stress breeds more stress.

Our example is biology student, Josh. He was stuck in the stress spiral, and he got really stressed when exams were approaching. When that happened, he avoided studying, started spiraling, and played video games online for hours into the night.

When Josh realized he had been wasting his time, he got even more stressed out about upcoming exams. Fortunately, Josh also realized that the only way to break the cycle is to just start studying. Once he had spent a few hours studying, his confidence increased because he was familiar with the material. This confidence meant he was less likely to procrastinate and instead spend more time studying. Good for him.

If you want to know how Josh so easily broke the spiral of avoiding his stressful studying session, you need to understand that **distress (the negative kind of stress) has three sources.**

#1: Sometimes distress has an *internal source*. These are the feelings, thoughts, and negative behaviors you might have that can cause negative stress. Internal events include fears and phobias, anxiety and worry about future events which you cannot control, perfectionistic or unrealistic expectations of yourself, and obsessive recurring thoughts, also known as ruminating. Often, we fantasize about hypothetical problems before they happen.

#2: Other times distress has a *behavioral source*. This is what Josh was experiencing. It happens when you display patterns in your behavior which put you at risk of entering the stress spiral. Behavioral patterns include procrastination, over-committing, and not being assertive when setting boundaries and saying, "No."

#3: Usually distress has a *power-struggle source*. This happens when you get stressed about things you can control like your lifestyle choice, not prioritizing your health and well-being, negative self-talk, and your beliefs. You also get stressed about things that seem out of your control like major life events such as a wedding or death, your physical environment, family, friends, colleagues, peers, daily chores, and your workload. These competing demands create a power-struggle for your attention.

Whether your stress is internal, behavioral, or from experiencing a power struggle, there will be triggers. and managing them is a proactive measure.

Recognizing your triggers or hot buttons is about knowing the events and situations that cause you to experience eustress and distress. If they can be managed, you can become the type of person who overcomes challenges that may arise.

Your hot button triggers might include:

Something you observe
e.g. someone you care about being treated badly

Something you think
e.g. believing that people are out to get you

Something you feel
e.g. feeling frustrated

Something you do
e.g. helping someone wihtout them expressing any gratitude

People will sometimes push your hot buttons. When pressed, they can impact what's important, undermine self-esteem, violate your values, and/or give you a feeling of loss or helplessness.

If you are aware of what your hot buttons are, you can prepare a response if one of them is triggered.

For this, you will need access to five captain entries that we discovered from a very rare and exclusive **Hot Button Response Manual.** This was left to us from our Maxme ancestors who were rumored to have sailed all our seven majestic seas.[xliv] In its pages you will unlock an understanding of the two basic responses to stress: Fight or Flight.

Captain's Log, Entry One:

Today a very large coconut fell from a tree and almost hit me. This made me realize that despite centuries of human evolution, there is an instinctive part of our brains that still exists.

After research, I found out it's called the amygdala and it drives our survival behaviors. When our amygdala is stimulated, it shuts down the rational part of our brain and releases hormones.

That release of hormones triggers a fight-or-flight response. This prepares your body to either stay and deal with a situation that is a perceived threat to your survival or to run away to safety. I ran, but my travel companion, Starbucks, tried hitting it with his wooden leg.

 Captain's Log, Entry Two:

Starbucks keeps talking about this idea that he must sell overpriced beverages, and it's irritating the crew. Like anyone in their right mind would ever pay ten times the cost of coffee, just to throw the cup away. He is such a dreaming lunatic.

Anyway, when they made fun of him about it, he might have overreacted when he broke our best mop and then threatened to spit on everyone's food. It just occurred to me that this is fight or flight in action. His amygdala went instantly irrational and, needless to say, he won't be winning any popularity contests anytime soon.

 Captain's Log, Entry Three:

Last night, the crew threw Starbucks in the brig. I guess they finally had enough, and they decided to give him a bit of time to cool down. When they locked the doors, he screamed and cried like a six-year-old who just lost his favorite teddy bear. Now the crew feels kind of guilty. We had no idea that his primitive brain would respond like that even though it wasn't at risk of actual danger. Could it be that he has a phobia? Better ask Second Mate, Claustro.

Captain's Log, Entry Four:

Claustro says that maybe Starbucks has a phobia of confined spaces and that's why he seemed terrified. Apparently, when you experience a rapid heartbeat and sweat excessively, these are signs that you might be having a panic attack. This makes sense.

Reminds me of the time when the crew was triggered once again by Starbucks. He absolutely insisted that instead of "cook" he preferred to be called a "barista." The crew boisterously laughed in his face.

Then the crew decided to put Starbucks on the spot and the boatswain asked him in front of everyone, "Why didn't your mother teach you better Italian?"

Immediately, Starbucks's pupils dilated, and he began to breathe rapidly. Enraged, he snapped, "Perhaps you'd prefer to go overboard?" In response, Starbucks' tunnel vision set in, he started to physically tremble, his muscles tensed, and his face looked flushed.

Truth is, I was more concerned about Starbucks's health after this incident. These physical symptoms seem to happen frequently for Starbucks, and our medical purser says he thinks they might be negatively affecting his well-being.

Regardless, I was glad to see that the next time he got enraged, Starbucks decided to seek my support to help him manage his reaction to stress. Maybe he is finally starting to see how negative behavior can be triggered by fight or flight.

 Captain's Log, Entry Five:

I'm thinking all the talks I have had with the crew about fight or flight over the years have helped us sail together on most days in peace. We sometimes have our terrible days too. This is understandable because the stress of the sea often brings out the worst in people's behavior. Either that, or they are tired of hearing me say, "Physical fight-or-flight responses can result in negative behaviors." I can't help my repetition.

I want my crew to know that if the fight comes out, like it does sometimes with Starbucks, we could see people snapping at others, raising their voices, or saying something hurtful. We can see the flight too. Everyone has done their fair share of avoiding conversations, leaving discussions without achieving a resolution, and insincerely not completing conversations as well.

All in all, occasionally these behaviors disrupt a few important navigation activities. But, in general, the crew is now aware of their responses to stress and what they can do to deal with it. They can decide that they won't let their instinct take over their rational thoughts when they are stressed.

What we can all learn from these entries is that you should embrace life's humor and be aware of your responses to stress. Otherwise, instead of pursuing your dreams, you might end up being thrown off a ship in the middle of the ocean.

Something might be causing you stress if:

 You get angry more easily

 You are having trouble sleeping when this is not normally a problem for you

 You are more irritable or withdrawn

 You want to be left alone

Your responses will have an impact on others, and it's always important to be aware of how your behaviors affect people's feelings and sense of worth - but particularly during times of conflict. Therefore, it's important to train your instincts during calm periods, so you can respond rationally during high-stress times. This training involves knowing the signs if something is causing you stress.

Thinking back over the last few months, what activities or topics triggered these kinds of responses? Once you become aware of your stressors, you can move your responses from instinctive to rational in a moment.

How? By breathing deeply and slowly. This slows your heart rate and moves your brain back to rational activities. Many people find comfort in visualizing a scene that gives them tranquility, like a beach, mountains, or a cozy chair next to a fireplace. Asking yourself questions about your triggers can also be helpful.

Either way, these are good techniques in the moment. Even better, you can prepare ahead of time by strengthening your resilience. As a result, you'll find handling these stressful moments even easier.

To strengthen your resilience, before reacting to someone, think, "This person is not a bad person, and I trust he is not trying to be disruptive." If need be, excuse yourself for a quick break from the situation to regroup. This can help you put a smile back on your face before returning. Often, this will show you that it wasn't as bad as you initially thought.

The knowledge and practice of this technique will help you build your resilience. In return, you will be better prepared to face difficult situations and stress that may hinder your long-term success. You can't stop challenges from coming into your life, but you can be proactive and put yourself in the best position to tackle them when they arise.

These techniques can help in the moment of flight or fight responses as well. In addition, self-advocating for resilience can help you be as prepared as possible for whatever life throws at you.

Resilience is important because it gives you the mechanisms to protect (preventative) against experiences that may be overwhelming, stressful, or difficult. It also gives you the strength to process and overcome (healing) hardship. It can even equip you with the ability to better deal with high-stress moments in life so you can stay in control. Once you gain your own handle on this, you can advocate for this skill in others, teaching them the techniques that have helped you.

Like Matt for example. He has low resilience. He gets easily overwhelmed and sometimes resorts to unhealthy coping methods such as task avoidance, self-destructive behavior, or abusing addictive substances. This guy could use our help.

Larry, on the other hand, is a highly resilient person. He can recover from setbacks, adapt to change, and keep going when the going gets tough. He does this by tapping into his strengths and he has a great support system that helps him work through his problems.

There are myriads of benefits for Matt to become more like Larry. According to the Resilience Institute, "Resilience practice increases your ability to focus on key priorities during challenging moments." For instance, Matt could experience significant personal or professional changes, difficult meetings, or competition from rivals.[xlv]

Resilience also increases your mental agility or how well your mind can adjust to new circumstances. For instance, meet our next example, Morgan.

Morgan loves the feeling of being resilient! It is like the friend Morgan never had. It is there for her when it matters most. With it, life seems easier for her, even when she works work with people facing big life changes.

Evidence of her resilience can be seen through her responses to unexpected events. It is clear Morgan has her situation under control and the ability to deal with people. Morgan is one smart cookie. She knows that if a friend or loved one needs help, resilience can save the day.

An example of a stressful situation to really drive this point home would be the time Morgan was working on a group assignment at a university. Enter the group situation from hell - where two people haven't met their commitments. This means the group's success is at risk. Ahhhhh!

If Morgan was a person of low resilience (*cough cough* like cook or barista Starbucks), she might become angry or lash out at members of the group. Since she is a person with high resilience, she chose to respond calmly. And just like that, having resilience gave her the ability to identify a reasonable solution to the situation. BOOM.

Don't feel bad if you aren't at her level yet. If you feel like you are constantly struggling because stress often brings out the worst in you, instead of feeling disappointed, you should know that experience counts.

People can and should use their previous negative experiences to learn about themselves and their responses. They can then decide how they want to do things in the future. The decision to use a proactive practice in a stressful situation can build your resilience. This is a choice we can all make.

If you are now looking for **10 proactive practices that will help strengthen your defenses and build your resilience** you have come to the right place.

#1: Improve the quality of your sleep. Sleep is the body's built in healing mechanism. When you are asleep, the brain packs away memories and processes the complex information you've encountered during the day. Adults typically need seven to nine hours of sleep every night.

After snoozing, you should note the amount of sleep and pay attention to how you feel. This will help you figure out your sweet spot. Also, pay attention to what caffeinated beverages you consume as they can affect sleep. Even though some people are more sensitive than others, caffeine makes it hard to fall asleep and stay asleep. To optimize your sleep, it's best to avoid stimulants that are caffeinated after early afternoon.

Your best feature should always be your big and sexy brain. You can take care of it by giving it time to rest before going to bed.

That means no devices in the bedroom and, ideally, reading to settle your mind before turning out the lights. Routine is also important for your brain in order to improve your quality of sleep, so try to go to bed at the same time and follow the same bedtime routine every night.

#2: Practice relaxation techniques. You wouldn't believe the thousands of approaches that are out there about how best to relax. The trick is to find something that works for you. Deep, focused breathing for 5-10 minutes is a good place to start. "Box breathing" is a simple exercise used by Navy SEALs in high-pressure situations.[xlvi]

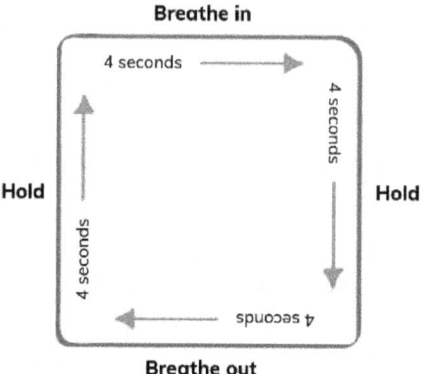

To practice box breathing you follow a specific, controlled pattern. First, breathe in for 4 seconds. Then, hold your breath for 4 seconds. Next, breathe out for 4 seconds. Finally, hold for 4 seconds. And repeat.

If you tried it and liked it, you might also like trying a meditation app. According to Jessica Migala, author at verywellmine.com,[xlvii] the seven best meditation apps are as follows:

Calm — Best overall

Insight Timer — Best budget

Headspace — Best for sleep

Ten Percent Happier Meditation — Best for beginners

Buddhify — Best guided

Unplug — Best for focus

Simple Habit — Best selection

If all else fails, you can always do some low-key activities that you just enjoy doing, like reading, listening to music, seeing friends, or going to the movies.

#3: Write a reflection/gratitude journal. This is an effective and fun way of focusing your mind on the positive things in your life. Creating a daily habit of writing in a gratitude journal can help you cope with negative situations by giving you perspective when you need it most. Every day, write about three to five things you are thankful for.

These could be small things like an unexpected smile from a shop assistant or big things like an upcoming holiday. Although it's not necessary, if you are a colorful marker and sticker addict, you can really have fun decorating as you build your reliance with this practice.

If you'd like, check out the one available in the #successishuman resource section on our website: www.maxme.com.au.

#4: Talk to someone you trust. The saying is true: A problem shared is a problem halved. Talking about your challenges with someone you trust has the effect of reducing how much stress it's causing you.

Your conversation doesn't need to result in solutions. The simple process of venting about your troubles will make you feel better. This practice can be particularly helpful if you can't do anything but accept a situation. A friend or mental health professional can help you work through your feelings by providing you with different perspectives.

#5: Exercise. We understand how appealing the sofa can seem but if you can muster up some energy we highly recommend participating in some endorphin-producing physical activity. Endorphins are the feel-good chemicals in our brains which also reduce our body's stress hormones.

Endorphins are responsible for the feelings of relaxation and optimism that a lot of people have at the end of a workout. Almost any type of exercise will help with this. Whether it's running, walking, cycling, tap dancing, yoga, or boxing, find out what works for you and make time for it in your weekly schedule.

#6: Eat a balanced diet. When you're busy or stressed, it's easy to resort to eating food that you know will make you feel gross later. There might be a time and place for sugary treats and fast food but try your best to aim for 80% of your meals to be nutritionally balanced. A balanced diet includes items from each food group: vegetables, fruits, grains, protein, and dairy.

Aim for whole grains in the morning. Throughout the day, incorporate lean proteins, dairy products, or substitutes that are fortified with calcium, three servings of vegetables, and two servings of fruit. If you are tempted by things like vending machines, bring healthy snacks with you when you travel and stay hydrated.

We think a balanced diet should really be called an all-day healthful way because it encourages better quality sleep and improves your brain function. It also helps stop bad food binges that can cause your energy to spike and then crash. We know this can be hard sometimes, but eating well will provide you with the energy you need to be a successful human.

#7: Don't rely on drugs or alcohol. If you are of legal age, a few drinks every now and then can be a fun way to blow off steam. But you should be aware of the potential impact substances can have on your ability to manage stress. This can be a dangerous path because using these items doesn't solve the root or cause of your stress.

Chronic drug or alcohol use makes stress worse and can result in mental health issues or worsen your existing conditions. We all know someone who struggles with this. If you think it might be you, there are several places to get support.[xlviii]

#8: Manage your time. An overwhelming workload or a looming deadline can be the cause of your stress. Here are a few quick tips: prioritize your tasks and work on the most important one first. Minimize distractions such as games, social media, chat, or anything else that draws you away from being productive.

Review your whole schedule and make sure you haven't over-committed to school/work, community, or other obligations. Remind yourself to focus and reset as necessary.

#9: Know your boundaries. These could be described as personal values because they set the standard of which kind of life you plan to live. Unclear or uncertain boundaries lead to confusion and stress, and this can throw your life out of balance.

Reinforce your boundaries by giving yourself permission to say, "No," as we talked about before. The practice of knowing your boundaries will build your resilience and protect your physical and emotional space.

#10: Be realistic. This is perhaps one of the best ways you can remain resilient. It's probably not a good idea to base your opinions off what you see on social media as it gives our society a whole lot of unrealistic information daily.

Lack of realism, particularly when you don't have much life experience, can make you feel unbalanced. Instead, try evaluating your thoughts by focusing on being realistic.

To accomplish this, practice leaning towards the best- case or worst-case scenarios so you can assess each situation. If you are pessimistic in your thinking (worst-case), adjust to become realistic (likely-case). Similarly, if you are optimistic (best-case), adjust accordingly.

These ten tips can help you build resilience since exploring a range of possible solutions allows you to gain control over your everyday stress. Advocates of resilience understand this, and they are open to experiencing new things that will help them grow. The more they master these concepts, the easier it will be for them to advocate for such skills to others. And the more they recognize the resulting advantages, the more excited they will be to share and advocate.

Plant and Grow a Mindset

There are many reasons why it can be hard to stick to good habits or develop new skills. But often, the biggest challenge is sitting within you. Your mind is a powerful thing. The stories you tell yourself, the things you believe about yourself, and your situations can either prevent change from happening or allow new skills to blossom.

Mindset is a person's way of thinking and the opinions they have, which then influence their choices and behavior. Carol Dweck, psychologist and author of *Mindset: The New Psychology of Success*, proposed that "Everything in your life comes down to your mindset, and there are only two types: Fixed and Growth."[xlix]

Fixed mindset people believe they are born with their abilities fixed and unchangeable. Whereas *growth mindset* people believe their abilities can be developed and strengthened overtime through hard work, positive thinking, and commitment.

Mindset plays a critical role in your success and how you cope with life's challenges. A growth mindset fosters motivation, resilience, and persistence. It opens new opportunities and if exhibited in a work environment, can make you better able to handle criticism.

It's evil twin, a fixed mindset, on the other hand, destroys these things and can leave you feeling stuck. Unless you enjoy being more likely to take things personally or giving up, better to listen to the kinds of attributes and traits a person with a growth mindset has.

People with a growth mindset are persistent with tasks, they have high levels of confidence when facing new things, they seek help from others, and they embrace challenges. They do this because they believe that intelligence and capability can be developed through the right attitude and perspective. These people are successful because of the way they think.

The story their growth mindset tells them:

- I can learn to do anything I want
- Challenges help me to grow
- Effort and attitude determine my abilities
- My intelligence and talent are ever improving
- I like to try new things
- I persist in the face of setbacks
- I learn to give and receive constructive criticism
- I'm inspired by the success of others

The story their fixed mindset tells them:

- I'm either good at it or I'm not
- My abilities are unchanging
- I don't like to be challenged
- I can either do it or I can't
- I stick to what I know
- When I'm frustrated, I give up
- I'm unable to handle criticism or feedback
- I'm threatened by success of others

Fixed mindset people are unsuccessful because they give up easily, they lack confidence in unfamiliar territory, and they avoid challenges and change. They often hide the struggles they experience from other people because they believe that intelligence is something you are born with and the ability to learn is limited by your natural born abilities.

The benefits of a growth mindset seem obvious, but most of us are guilty of having a fixed mindset in certain situations throughout our lives. That can be dangerous because a fixed mindset can often prevent important skills and growth. This could sabotage your health and happiness.

We need not look any further to see what having a fixed mindset looks like because we can once again rely on the classic childhood story of The Tortoise and the Hare.[l] Remember how the hare was so damn confident that he would win in a race against the tortoise that he stopped in the middle of it and took a nap?

Well, as we know, the tortoise kept plodding along. He believed he had a chance of winning the race. When the hare eventually woke up, he ran as fast as he could, but it was too late. The tortoise already won.

A lesson we can learn from the story is that the hare had a fixed mindset. He believed that his innate ability and speed meant that he would always win in whatever he did.

The tortoise had a growth mindset because he was not afraid of failure. He agreed to race the hare in the first place because he believed that if he worked hard and persevered through his challenges, he might have a chance at winning.

Another example, this time human, of what a fixed mindset looks like is provided to us by learning about a new person. Meet Winston.

He is a bit stubborn. By the end of this example, you'll be glad he is not in front of you because you may want to slap him. Winston, does not believe what Jim Rohn, author, entrepreneur, and motivational speaker, suggests that people need to tell themselves, "Work harder on yourself than you do on your job."[li]

This is clear because today Winston really frustrated his entire group in math class. When given his part of the project he insisted he couldn't do it because as he says it, "I'm not a math person."

This is just an easy excuse for him to avoid practicing the problems. Does this guy really believe he is incapable of learning math? He really thinks he is the type of person who doesn't need it. Seriously?

If he had a growth mindset, he would be willing to try. Oh, Winston, why can't you just become the kind of person who is comfortable saying "This is a skill I'm not good at...yet."

It's important to know that in times of challenges, Winston has a choice to embrace a growth mindset and you have a choice to help support him. So, what can you do to make the group feel happier about his company? Encourage the group to think positively about maximizing their own potential.

Successful humans demonstrate their growth mindset by advocating for positivity for themselves and for their teams. Positivity allows people to overcome their challenges rather than avoiding them, learn from criticism rather than ignoring it, and find inspiration in the success of others rather than feeling threatened.

Practicing positivity begins by thinking about what you want and how to get it. This will in return allow you to feel happier and in greater control. Your beautiful brain will then release endorphins or hormones that will give you a feeling of well-being. As a result, you develop a positive attitude towards work and life.

You might be thinking that having a positive attitude is easier said than done. In this case, you should know that while it might seem to come naturally to some people more than others, it is a skill that anyone can develop and grow.

To prove this, we have developed a list of ten different ways you can encourage and advocate for positive thinking which supports a growth mindset.

#1: Be aware. Have you ever noticed that when you are having a bad day, your body language shows it? You slump over, you don't make eye contact with others, and do things like frown when you are feeling uncomfortable.

Try to be consciously aware of your better-days and my not-so-good days. If you're feeling mildly unhappy, avoid posting on social media. We think it's called the "happiness reel." It makes you think people are out there experiencing life and you are just sad. TRUST US. Online, most people appear to have their shit together, and that's just not the case.

Instead, don't allow technology or outside sources of any kind to stop you from having a growth mindset. Recognize that your environment and circumstances do not control your mind or your reactions. Positive thinking is as much about your body as it is your brain.

Non-verbal communication matters. Observe yourself, and as soon as you catch yourself giving into a physical indicator like a nervous tick, straighten up. Holding your body in a powerful pose makes it easier to positively communicate with others.

#2: Adjust your thinking. Imagine this. You slept in and missed the train. You are now running late. When you get to your destination, someone bumps into you, and you drop your paperwork. What a morning.

Fortunately, a friend sees what happened and he apologies on behalf of the person who bumped into you. Then he smiles, reminds you that the day will get better, and helps you pick up your things. You eventually get to your meeting on time, right before the presenter walks in.

As you sit in the chair waiting, you are probably thinking about one of two things. The problems you faced getting to the meeting or the helpfulness of the person who assisted you. You are either the person who wished they stayed home, or you are the person who is happy you didn't miss any of the lecture. You can either concentrate on the positive or focus on the negative. The choice is yours.

A person who adjusts their thinking knows that what's happened, has happened. And what will come, is yet to come. Consciously choosing to focus on the positive moments in the present begins the process of re-framing your thoughts. This outlook will cultivate a way of thinking that is grateful and open rather than negative and closed off.

#3: Mind your language. What you say stems from what you are thinking. We all know people who need to think before they speak. The words you choose, both in conversation and in your own mind, have a deep impact on how you think. To develop positive thinking, you need to know that every negative sentence that comes out of your mouth is a command you give your brain towards negativity.

Think about this next time you are having a stressful day. Instead of saying, "This is such a bad day," try something like, "The first half of the day had its challenges." The first statement clearly portrays a negative mindset, while the latter portrays an optimistic statement that will make you feel better.

#4: Spend time with positive people. We surround ourselves with different types of people and some can easily lift your mood while others will drain you of your confidence.

Eleanor Roosevelt, former first lady of the United States once said, "No one can make you feel inferior without your consent."[lii] This is important to remember as you consider the people you hang out with. If you think certain people are sending off negative vibes that make you feel less valuable, you should distance yourself from them as much as possible.

It might not be practical to completely cut them out of your life, especially in a work environment, but you can limit your interactions with them. A recent study by *The Current Opinion in Psychology*, revealed that having positive friendships significantly reduces stress. Which is why it is so important to spend as much time as you can with people who have a positive attitude towards life.[liii]

#5: View failure in a different light. Don't list all the mistakes you've made. This can lead to some unhealthy thoughts of what might have been. Instead, consider failure as a time to apply extra effort to improve yourself and your results.

Do not remain in the facade that you are always right, that you are always in control, or that you are not capable enough to seize an opportunity. Failure is what happens; it's the understanding you can learn from it that matters. If it helps, you can look at failure with positivity just like Thomas A. Edison, who once said, "I have not failed. I just found 10,000 ways that won't work."[liv]

Either way, when you fail in one situation it's perfectly okay and it does not mean you have failed as a person. What is not okay is having a fear of failure and, as a result, not trying new things that could improve your life.

#6: View challenges as opportunities. The word "failing" can be replaced with the word "learning" as could the word "failure" with "opportunity." When you make a mistake or fall short of a goal, you can apply what you have learned from your experience towards your next big idea.

In 1919, Walt Disney was fired from the Kansas City Star Newspaper. His editor thought he, "Lacked imagination and had no good ideas."[lv] So how did Walt bounce back and prove his boss wrong? He literally created the happiest place on Earth, which was none other than the world's most famous theme park that inspires millions of children and adults alike.

Having a growth mindset means that you must become the type of person who actively seeks opportunities for self-improvement. You do this because you believe in achieving your greater sense of purpose. As you recognize the importance of this, advocating for it will be easy.

#7: Keep learning and aspiring. Eartha Kitt had the right idea when she said, "I am learning all the time. The tombstone will be my diploma."[lvi] You are never done learning in life. It is never too late or too early to discover interesting things to learn or fascinating subjects to study.

It is always a good idea to devote your time and energy towards becoming the kind of person you aspire to be. The same applies for devoting time to practicing growth mindset skills.

Growth-minded people know how to constantly create new goals to keep themselves stimulated even if other people discourage it. This was certainly the case when you think of Albert Einstein. The word *genius* comes to mind when we think about his legacy.

But did you know that Einstein didn't speak full sentences until he was five years old? His teachers thought he was slow. In 1895, Albert Einstein's teacher said to his father, "It doesn't matter what he does, he will never amount to anything."[lvii]

He went on to revolutionize science's understanding(s) of the world, taking physics beyond its Newtonian view by developing the theory of relativity. He won the Nobel Prize AND influenced all aspects of life and culture. Not too shabby for someone who would never amount to anything. Learning and aspiring are timeless and boundless.

#8: Focus on the bigger picture. It's where we end up that matters. Focus on where you want to be. In agreement is Marcel Pagnol, who once said, "The reason people find it so hard to be happy is that they always see the past better than it was, the present worse than it is, and the future less resolved than it will be."[lviii]

Try to smile about what might be and adhere to a few things that make your thoughts of the future more delightful. If you stumble in your progress, remember that learning takes time. Advocates of human skills keep the big picture in mind and continue to try.

You will encounter setbacks, obstacles, and interesting challenges. You will also encounter achievements and opportunities. Keeping your mind positive is a process you can work on daily. This is exactly how it is meant to be.

Successful humans advocate for mindfulness, positive thinking, and having a growth mindset because they know the worth of view from the top will be breathtaking.

#9: Smash through self-limiting thoughts. We are not really conditioned to think positively about ourselves, and we tend to focus on the things we are not good at in the spirit of self-protection. Self-limiting thoughts are the sucklings of your potential.

Those thoughts say you can't do things you are more than capable of. They tell you that you are going to fail. They stop you from trusting yourself and taking positive risks. They stop you from growing because self-limiting thoughts have a detrimental ripple effect.

Mahatma Gandhi said, "Your thoughts become your words, your words become your actions, your actions become your habits, your habits become your values, your values become your destiny."[lix] Therefore, it's important to get your thoughts where you need them to be.

Successful humans openly believe that they can live their best life and discover what they are capable of. You have so much to offer. Believe in this truth. Actively advocate for such thinking in yourself and others.

#10: Play to win (verses playing not to lose). This is a subtle concept in its difference but HUGE in its potential impact. Both approaches get the same result, a win. But the path to getting to the win feels very different.

Playing to win requires a growth mindset. It means that you choose to play with an attitude that is open to possibilities. You will be more likely to feel energized, hopeful, and as you push yourself, you might even have fun.

Playing to lose feels quite different. The fear of losing is so strong that all you can do is not lose. Your attitude is one of fear and protection at all costs, but it doesn't have to be. Successful humans know that winning and losing is a part of life that can either be played defensively or freely. Advocate for such thinking.

Post this in a place where you can remind yourself to have a growth mindset every day. (Remake it with fun colors, if you'd like, and don't forget to share it with us).

Growth Mindset

Be aware.
Adjust your thinking.
Mind your language.
Spend time with positive people.
View failure in a different light.
View challenges as opportunities.
Keep learning and aspiring.
Focus on the bigger picture.
Smash through self-limiting thoughts.
Play to win (versus not to lose).

Armed with these ten different ways you can advocate for positive thinking. Your growth mindset should feel secure by now. But don't get too comfortable.

Maintaining a positive mindset is critical to your success and how you cope with life challenges. Which is why we are relieved that in times of need, we can always rely on our allies. Enter kindness and gratitude.

Buy Into the K & G Fluff Stories

Kindness and gratitude seem like such fluffy words, don't they? We like to think of them as more tangible. They are the items you need in your mindful arsenal as you look through the lenses of success and struggle in this world.

Everyone views our world differently, and that view can vary from time to time. As part of that, people wonder and worry about regression and advancement. That's why you need kindness and gratitude. That fluff cleans the lenses so people can see more opportunities.

Being a kind person is about more than doing nice things. It encompasses actions that are motivated by compassion and empathy. It can be shown in many ways, such as forgiving your friend, giving directions to someone who looks lost, or donating your water jug to a traveling adventurer.

You can also be nice without necessarily considering or caring for someone's well-being, like opening a door for a capable stranger, for example. Acts such as these are done to benefit the other person, not just to be polite or to get something in return.

On the other hand, being an empathic and compassionate person means you have the ability to feel understanding towards the circumstances of others or yourself. Trying to understand others without judgement is key to expressing kindness.

Before trying to understand other people, you should know that successful people are, first and foremost, kind, empathic, and compassionate to themselves. This might sound selfish, but it's not. They understand that their thoughts and feelings can either lift or dampen themselves, which leads to raising or lowering the spirit of others around them. They consider negative opinions and self-criticism to be roadblocks of kindness to everyone, including themselves.

By knowing that kindness starts with you, you should also know that being an advocate of kindness can be seen through what you do, your ACTIONS:

A — Advocate for showing someone kindness even though it can be difficult.

C — Cooperation isn't about the other person, it's about who you choose to be at that moment.

T — Take the high road by checking yourself first. This means no gossiping or refraining from making a sarcastic comment that could hurt someone's feelings.

I — If something seems like an unkind thing to do, stop and ask yourself if it's necessary.

O — Only your mindful actions will help you to recognize and avoid moments of unkindness.

N — Not only is kindness ultimately a key contributor to happiness but acting with kindness is a win-win outcome for everyone in your life.

S — Spread this thinking to others with the intention of making a positive impact.

Above all, practicing kindness as a skill is more than just an action and a reaction. It should also include a positive emotion that serves a biological purpose, to increase feelings of enjoyment and enthusiasm. So, this means that taking a moment to be kind to someone else will have a positive impact on yourself.

In addition to your actions, kindness can be seen by how it is received. This should include saying "thank you" to the person who has helped you.

Gratitude is being thankful and showing appreciation for the kindness paid to you. It should result in returning kindness to others.

Gratitude is also about appreciating what you have. Such as family, friends, and health, instead of always reaching for something new in hopes it will make you happier. Thinking that you can't feel satisfied until every physical and material need you have is met is unrealistic. That's why it's important to count your blessings.

Not to sound bitter, but sadly, showing appreciation has become a lost art. Too many people feel they are entitled to what they have or what they want. Gratitude helps you focus on what you have instead of what you lack. Although it may feel contrived at first, this mental state grows stronger with use and practice. Successful humans advocate for shifting their minds to focus on what they have instead.

Do yourself a favor. Take some time each day to express gratitude for each and everything that comes your way. Keep a list for one week about every good thing that happens regardless of how small the gesture: a funny email, a phone call from a friend, a smile from a stranger, for instance. At the end of the week, you'll be astounded at how much you have to be grateful for.

It's amazing how practicing kindness and gratitude naturally makes you an advocate for them without even trying and they happen to be contagious. Not the bad kind of contagiousness that leaves you feverish and drained, but the kind that provides you with a sense of pride because you acted thoughtfully towards others. In other words, practicing both as skills have the potential to boost your confidence and give happiness to yourself and those around you.

You never know just how big an impact practicing kindness and gratitude can have on those around you. For instance, Orly Wahba, founder of Life Vest Inside, started a non-profit organization with a mission to encourage people to embrace the incredible power of giving and recognize that in times of hardship, "Kindness, like a life vest, keeps the world afloat."[lx]

Her actions captured national attention when she created a short film called "Kindness Boomerang." When it went viral, it received more than 20 million views. In gratitude, the response was coverage by media outlets such as Ad Week, IBTimes, and CBS News.

As a result of its broadcasting, the impact was a Kindness Movement. This is undeniable as evidence that everyone can be positively affected by acts of kindness.

Just think about it. If there was a commercial that boasted about the positive physical benefits of kindness and gratitude, everyone would buy the product the company was trying to showcase. Imagine the pitch:

Do you want a stronger immune system?
To be less bothered by aches and pains?
Lower your blood pressure?
Increase your interest in health and well-being?
And provide you with better quality sleep?
Then ACT NOW and buy Gratitude and Kindness today!

People would be interested. Even more so if they knew the psychological benefits of kindness and gratitude, such as higher levels of positive emotions including joy, pleasure, optimism, and naturally, happiness.

Along with having an interest in kindness and gratitude, you need to become an observer of opportunities for more K & G fluff. If not, you could miss something important that is happening right in front of your eyes.

To help you learn how to observe kindness and gratitude opportunities, we brought along an old storybook that we obtained from a friend of ours. Enjoy.

Once upon a time... Archeologist and explorer Indie Bones was somewhere in the sweltering Amazon jungle when he began his quest for K & G fluff. As legend has it, obtaining it can lead a person to opportunities beyond their wildest dreams.[lxi]

The need for this journey dawned upon him rather accidentally when he was careless in packing his travel gear. He had forgotten his thermos, and now he couldn't ensure that he would be adequately hydrated throughout his journey "Damn," he muttered, through his thirst.

After what seemed like hours of dry mouth when all seemed lost, he saw an elderly man sitting beneath a large tree who offered him a drink. In appreciation, Indie kindly offered to help the man gather firewood even though it was usually something he loathed doing. The man was grateful for Indie's strength, and this gesture engendered mutual respect.

As they worked, Indie noticed that the man appeared to be wealthy. His clothes were made of fine linens, and his tent was adorned with shiny decor. Regardless, both of them spent the day smiling, and it was clear each had something to offer the other.

That night over a roaring fire pit, the man told Indie about how kindness and gratitude can lead to happiness. His eyes grew wide when he spoke of his life before he built the miraculous fortune that forged his legacy. He encouraged Indie to pursue K & G fluff. "Buy before you begin," the old man advised, "you should decide what compassion and empathy means to you."

Indie never really thought about that before. What he did know was that, from this point on, he must be open to giving and receiving kindness so he could feel more connected to other people. The following morning Indie felt good about himself and left with a jug of water slung over his broad shoulders.

From that day forward, Indie practiced gratitude and kindness. Eventually he lived a life better than he ever imagined and died a happy man. The End.

I bet you're wondering why we ended our story without telling you what compassion and empathy meant to Indie or about the specific steps he took to obtain kindness and gratitude after he observed them. We decided not to list them just yet because it doesn't really matter. For now, what's important is that you learn from the moral of the story.

If you want more K & G fluff, you must decide to be the type of person who is open to kindness and gratitude yourself. Successful humans are advocates of sharing this truth.

So how can you begin? By noticing the small moments and by harnessing the power of observation to act accordingly. Introducing these actions into your life will improve your attention, make you feel satisfied in your relationships, decrease your stress, and increase your appreciation.

Observation makes Actions more Effective

Observation happens when you see, hear, or notice something or someone. It is a deliberate thought process and with it, you can gain information. This information can make your intended actions more effective.

For example, let's say you're trying to practice kindness from the last chapter. Your action might be to do something thoughtful for another person. In this case, we will call that person Linda.

So, you go to the coffee shop and buy Linda a latte. Then you observed that even though she seemed grateful, she didn't drink it. When asked about it, she tells you that she doesn't drink coffee in any form. She does, however, love bagels and cream cheese. Thanks to observation, you just learned the more effective action you should take to be thoughtful of Linda. That seems easy, *right?*

Indeed, it does. Observing a friend not drinking coffee and then acting next time with a suggested bagel is simple stuff. The deliberate thought process of observation, however, can be tricky to master. *Why?*

Well, first of all, observations can be facts and they can also be opinions. Facts are those things that are true for everybody. For example, it's a fact that currently, it is officially recognized that there are seven continents: Africa, Antarctica, Asia, Australia, Europe, North America, and South America.

Opinions are beliefs based on personal perspectives. They are subjective rather than objective. They often involve judgements and biases. An example of this might be observing and then deciding on whether a teacher is good at their job after you attend several of his or her classes.

Whether in fact or opinion, you can begin practicing deliberate observation by developing better observation habits. This involves actively watching things with an open, focused, and curious mind. This begins by changing your perspective.

Most of the time, we think of observation as something we do with our eyes. The truth is, all five of our senses can be used to make observations - sight, hearing, taste, touch, and smell. Often the missing piece of the observation puzzle is registering and paying attention.

When you are mindful, you pay attention to what is going on inside and outside of you in your environment. Paying attention to what's happening outside involves sight, sound, smell and/or taste. Paying attention to what's happening inside involves your feelings, thoughts, emotions, sensations, and impulses.

As you develop and improve your powers of observation, you may find that certain senses develop more than others. The key to becoming a better observer is to exercise all your senses so that no one sense becomes dominant. That would result in biased observations.

You can start by actively paying attention to one of your senses in the present moment. Then transition between each of your senses one at a time to make sure you're exercising and tuning in to all of them. It's a bit like doing exercises that isolate different muscle groups to make sure each gets the time and attention they need to grow and work even better together.

Let's try. Go to a coffee shop.

When you arrive, notice what is in your environment and write your responses in the boxes.

COFFEE SHOP OBSERVATION ACTIVITY

My Environment

I can
see...

I can
hear...

I can
smell...

I can
taste...

COFFEE SHOP OBSERVATION ACTIVITY

Inside my head

What are my feelings about this place?

What are my thoughts about this place?

What are my emotions about this place?

What are my sensations about this place?

What are my impulses about this place?

Whether you are in a coffee shop or elsewhere, successful people practice paying attention so they can get better at being deliberately observant. They are observant when they are watching people, situations, and events. Then they think about what they have observed before they respond. This helps them gain a better perspective on things and puts them in the best position to decide how to effectively act.

Observation can be a useful human skill. It can help you to better understand why someone might exhibit challenging behavior. It can also improve how you practice kindness and gratitude.

Those who utilize deliberate observation use the information they have gathered to inform their actions because they understand that their actions can lead to achieving their goals. They can then easily advocate for this skill in those around them, understanding its impact.

Set Goals with a Focused Intention

As we learned in the last chapter, acting after observation is where the magic happens. Charles Eisenstein, author, and public speaker once said, "There is a time to act, and a time to wait, to listen, to observe. Then understanding and clarity can grow. From understanding, action arises that is purposeful, firm, and powerful."[lxii]

If you want this type of powerful magic to work for you, it's all about acting with focused intention after observation. These kinds of actions move your life forward towards your goals. Setting and achieving goals is an important life skill worth advocating, for yourself and others.

Acting with focused intention means you commit to what you want. You commit to an outcome that is important to you and create an unshakeable determination to accomplish it. That means you say no to slacking and no to excuses so you can have a real chance to turn an idea into something truly meaningful and lasting.

You can demonstrate a focused intention by being highly selective with your limited time and energy. With your time and energy, your goals should be a priority over other things. This involves removing distractions from your life that are holding you back.

Author Nir Eyal's perspective is that, "Distraction, it turns out, isn't about the distraction itself; rather, it's about how we respond to it."[lxiii] Therefore, it's necessary to say no to things that don't improve you. Then you will become the type of person who is more open to saying yes to things that do.

When you have a focused intention, you say yes to increasing the odds of observing things that others might miss. This includes patterns, mistakes, and new opportunities. You also say yes to an environment where interruptions are minimized so you'll be free to take notice of the things that matter to you.

Though intention is important, intention without a goal is meaningless. Tremendous growth and learning occur at the intersection of both.

Focused intentioned people are aware of the importance of staying balanced, practicing resilience, their growth mindset, how kindness and gratitude can positively contribute to their lives, and how their observations can contribute to their meaningful actions. But these skills are not the only things that contribute towards their achievements. Above all, successful humans advocate for the ownership of their goals.

Take Pablo Picasso as an example. Although he lived during a different time, "Our goals," he exclaimed, "can only be reached through a vehicle of plan, in which we must fervently believe, and upon which we must vigorously act. There is no other route to success."[lxiv]

This timeless advice pinpoints why you should be an advocate for owning the process of planning the activities required to reach your desired outcome. This process is called goal setting.

Goal setting is one of the most powerful and effective ways of working out what you want to achieve and then setting out how you are going to achieve it. It is engaging in the process of goal setting, developing the approach to achieve those goals, outlining and prioritizing your tasks and activities, and then creating a clear roadmap on how to accomplish those goals. With this understanding, you can focus on the goal and work effectively to achieve it without randomly trying things and hoping they will make a difference.

Establishing goals is the first step towards action, and it will play a fundamental role in the development of the techniques involved in setting your achievable outcomes. This is the target you should aim to reach.

Think about it. If you travel, your goal is to take a trip. If you throw a party, your goal is to have an event. If you need to take a test, your goal is to pass it. If you are working on a team, your goal is to divide the work. Of course, you can do these things without any goal setting, but you're more likely to run into issues that could have been avoided.

Sometimes the effect of not goal setting might be minor or barely noticeable, and sometimes it can completely derail you from achieving much of anything. Many people neglect to set goals and then get disappointed and discouraged when they don't get what they want. Or they look back on what they could have achieved, and they regret not putting goals in place.

Effective goal setting provides people who are busy a much-needed clarity on what needs to get done based on their goals. And really, who doesn't want to make the most out of the time they have? Who doesn't want to spend more time focusing on the things that make them happy and fulfilled?

So why is goal setting often neglected? Because people think "What's the point of goal setting when things could change anyway?" or the more whinny "I can't control everything."

And they are sometimes correct since flexibility can be an asset when things change. But goal setting is important because it helps you identify what you want, and the necessary steps needed to reach your intended goals.

This doesn't have to be hard or boring and not all goals are equal. Some goals are linked to things you must do, like filing your tax return on time or submitting a project by the deadline. Other goals are connected to what you want to achieve for yourself. These might be personal goals such as running a marathon or learning a language.

Rather than relying on chance or fate, goal setting provides you with a path with milestones to measure progress. There is never only one path, but goal setting will help you figure out the right path for you. Navigating a path to achieving their goals is certainly something that successful people do.

Regardless of the type of goals you have, you must set them and commit to doing what it takes to achieve them. When you do, makes sure to write them down and tell someone about them. Why? This handy dandy study explains that aspect of goal setting.

Psychology professor Dr. Gail Matthews, at the Dominican University in California, led a study on goal setting with nearly 270 participants. The results? People are 42 percent more likely to achieve their goals if they write them down. If they tell someone else, their chances of success increase to almost 80%![lxv] That's impressive.

In addition, connect with the reason why your goals are your goals, and this will help you to commit. Aim for goals that stretch you but are achievable and measurable. Sure, be realistic, but challenge yourself. Don't let fear cause you to sell yourself short. You can do it. Keep going. Success is not by accident. It's a combination of intended actions carefully taken one step, towards one goal, at a time.

Here are **five goal setting actions you should advocate for in your life and those you influence:**

#1: Ask questions so you'll choose the right goals. Questions help you achieve your purpose. When you take the time and effort to ask them, it enables you to focus on your goals and desired outcomes. It's about fast-forwarding through all the bullshit in your life and instead considering more about what you want your future to look like.

Asking them gives you a better idea of your destination so you can take steps in the right direction. This is sometimes called thinking with the end in mind. Knowing this can be a strong source of motivation for you.

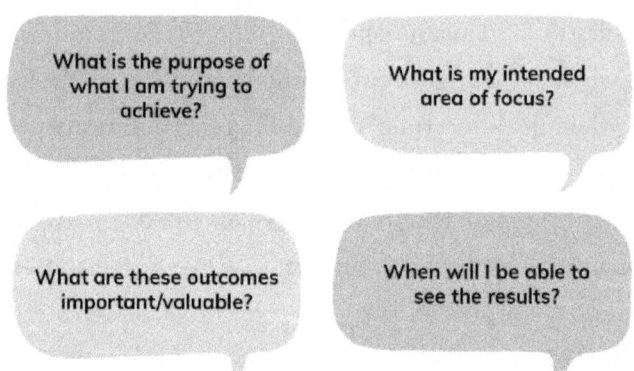

#2: Strategically narrow down your goals. Now that you've got a goal in mind, creating a strategy so you can achieve your goal can be daunting. It can sometimes be difficult to determine how to begin. Take a minute to think about how you can use your time efficiently.

Efficiently managing your time means you concentrate on your most important priorities. As in many areas in your life, less is more. This applies to setting your goals too. By focusing on fewer plans at a time, you will have more impact.

Studies indicate that focusing on multiple things at the same time, some people call it multi-tasking, reduces your productivity by 40%.[lxvi] Goals are great, but if you have too many of them, or are working on too many at the same time, you can become distracted, demotivated, or just overwhelmed.

Failing to manage your time efficiently may cause unnecessary stress and reduce your effectiveness. Remember, being busy is not the same as being effective and your time must be adjusted accordingly.

So, begin by identifying the most important goals. Then, you need to efficiently take focused actions in a reasonable timeframe. *But how?*

#3: Break your goals down into small goals. These are actionable tasks that you can achieve during a day's time.

Imagine you had to (for whatever reason) eat a piece of cake the size of an elephant. How can this be done? One bite at a time. You get the point. Taking things one small step at a time makes the bigger task seem more achievable.

This process of breaking goals down will help you understand all the smaller actions and activities that are involved in achieving your desired outcome. It also helps you create a timeline to get things done. A bonus is that by creating a series of realistic mini goals along the way helps you feel a constant sense of achievement which will encourage you to work harder.

As you work, keep in mind that what works for you might be different than for someone else. Maybe you set yourself calendar reminders to check your progress. Other ideas include putting post-it notes on a wall as a reminder or using an online tracking tool. It's really a matter of finding what works best for you.

If you find things are not working, no worries; it's okay to stop and refocus. Better to adjust to a new direction than to stick with one that's not getting you where you need to be.

Regardless of whether your goal is to eat a massive piece of cake or to own a thriving company someday, you need to start somewhere. Then you need to track your progress to know that your small goals are leading you in the right direction, which is our next point.

#4: Create a plan for how to achieve and measure your goals. Decide how you will monitor and evaluate your progress. Having ways to check yourself before you wreck yourself isn't a new idea. It's all about progress monitoring and taking stock of where things are on a regular basis.

This is called evaluation and it provides you with an opportunity to reflect and learn from what you have already done. Then you can assess the results and the effectiveness of your actions and adjust them before continuing. This is a way people can inform themselves for their future actions.

Naturally, you will need some sort of tool to do this. Your tool can help you be the type of person who monitors their progress rather than the type who has good intentions but does not follow through on what they say they are going to do.

Your plan isn't going to keep track of itself...it needs to be measured to make sure you get there. You need to regularly do this to ensure your goal stays relevant and real. Keep checking in to make sure it is still achievable. This involves taking note of what you're doing such as your behaviors and actions. It also includes the resulting changes, or outcomes, and how those changes compare to what you're aiming to achieve or target.

Life happens. If your goals aren't getting where you need them to be, you will need to make necessary adjustments to make sure you don't just keep acting without intended focus.

#5: Revise your goals as need be. We are not sure if anything feels better than doing a spontaneous happy dance because everyone got their act together and killed it. For other times, thank goodness for the revision process in goal setting. This can help you (re)define your true goal.

You might start out believing you want a particular goal. Then you break it down, ask questions, and really examine the outcome and what's needed to make it happen. This process of exploration, analysis, and reflection can help you gain deeper insight into what you want and/or how you want to approach it.

Maybe upon further reflection, you see that the pursuit of this goal and/or the path to get there doesn't align with your values. Revision can be a great way to avoid investing time in an outcome you didn't want or taking an approach that is inconsistent with your strengths. And sometimes along the path to the goal, you simply realize it isn't working the way you'd hoped.

Revision of goals is an essential process. You will have to work hard during revision, but this is the only way of getting anywhere. As you revise your goals, ask yourself reflective questions such as:

When it comes to revising your goals, things to consistently keep asking yourself include:

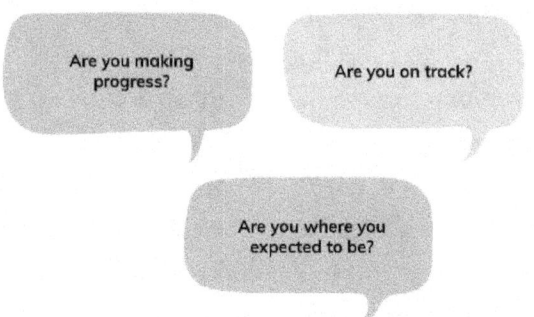

Along with these questions, the five goal setting actions, and an intended focus in your arsenal, you are well on your way to becoming an advocate for human skills that feed your success or you can share with others to feed theirs. But now it's time to get real.

Some goals will be exciting and with others, you might find it hard to stay focused. Staying committed is something you will have to work on too.

Commit to Your Goals

Commitment to your goals matters. Being a good starter but not a good finisher will make it very hard to obtain the skills you need for both a successful career and a meaningful life. We often hear the reasons why people give up are things like, "It wasn't meant to be, something more important came up, it was beyond me, it wasn't fun anymore, or it's all too hard." Blah blah blah. What a load of crap.

Commitment means you know achieving your goals will be hard, but with courage, persistent focus, strong will, discipline, and a little faith, you decide to try anyway. Bet you are wondering how you can remain committed to your goals, and important human skill to possess. You can by creating "calls to action" which reinforces what you want and keeps you focused on what you need to do.

Here are **seven practices to build "calls to action" so you can commit to your goals every day:**

#1: Create success habits. Be the person who sets goals and achieves them. Tell your old habits and your comfort zone that you are a new person now and you won't be plagued by excuses that have prevented you from achieving your targets and dreams.

Since a habit is an action that is repeated daily, you can purposefully develop habits by choosing an action and performing it regularly. Consider advocating for habits that are common for successful people, such as challenging yourself, making use of feedback, and setting goals.

Maybe you might decide you are going to commit to writing in a gratitude journal every night for a week. Once you achieve that, set a goal to do it for a month. This way you can build on your own success.

#2: Set routines. Routines are habits in order. They might seem boring, but they may be just the things you need to stay focused. Make sure your routines are positive, realistic, and something you look forward to following, rather than dreading. Figure out what routines work for you. Practice them and adjust them if they start feeling demotivating. Ask yourself what is important to you and the best time to do each task on your action plan.

By establishing routines, you will work more consistently, which will deliver better results, not just for your goals but in all aspects of your life. But be flexible in your routines as well. A good example is running to stay fit. If the weather turns bad for an extended period and you can't run, do you have another form of exercise to do as part of your daily routine? Always have a plan B otherwise you will get stuck. Remember routines are a balancing act too.

#3: Stay inspired. Sometimes your motivation needs a little nudge in the right direction. Finding what or who inspires you can be a great way to keep on track with your goals.

Visualize your goals.
Positive imagery is a powerful way to remain inspired. Think about your goals every day. Imagine how you feel when you have taken a step towards a goal or reached it. Use these images and feelings to motivate yourself.

Stay positive.
Encourage yourself with positive self-talk. If you're the sort of person who doesn't like to fail but then tells yourself a task is too difficult, chances are you either won't even attempt it or you'll fail if you do try.

Remove limits.
If you tell yourself a task is a challenge and an opportunity to test your skills or learn new ones, you're creating a positive situation for yourself in which you are not limited by your own apprehension.

What are some ways you can stay inspired?

> **Work with others.**
> It's easier to get and stay inspired when you're working with others who have similar goals or someone who will motivate you to stay on track.

> **Reward yourself.**
> Every time you meet an objective, stop and celebrate your achievement because you will know you're advancing in the right direction. Treat yourself to recognize what you have achieved. You deserve it.

#4: Look at the big picture. Staying on track is hard. Reconnecting to the purpose behind the goal and the real reason why it's important to you can be enough to refocus you.

Realize that any setbacks are temporary. You are not doomed to fail just because you have lost sight of your goal or because your motivation has diminished. Don't give up. Remember long-term goals are just a series of smaller objectives.

#5: Stay accountable. Accountability is when you take responsibility for your actions. Self-motivation for this can be extremely difficult. It can be helpful to surround yourself with powerful words and people that inspire you.

Remember that person you talked to about your goal? Ask them to keep you motivated and on track. Plan to check in with them regularly so you can stay accountable.

#6: Stay on course. To stay committed to your goals, you need to work hard on nurturing them and making sure they stay on the top of your thoughts. As legendary George Lucas says, "Dreams are extremely important. You can't do it unless you can imagine it."[lxvii] After all, your imagined goals are what keep you motivated- they're your goals so it's important to constantly remember that.

#7: Revisit your goals frequently. Goal setting is not just about creating a list. It's about revising your list as circumstances change and evolve. Adjust them as required.

In time, these tips will become second nature. They will help you commit to your goals even if you feel like you are juggling a heap of commitments simultaneously. For times like these, there are two methods you can use to prioritize your commitments so you can commit to your goals.

On a side note, if you are reading this first thing in the morning, these methods pair well with a hot beverage, enjoy.

Method one sounds obvious, but you should be ranking your priorities on what matters as opposed to what you would enjoy doing. **The Eisenhower Matrix** is a useful tool if you are new to prioritizing.

As the name suggests, former US president Dwight Eisenhower developed it. This approach can help you maintain a home, when you are studying, or in your career. It's a simple four-quadrant box that helps identify what you should be working on, and it looks like this:

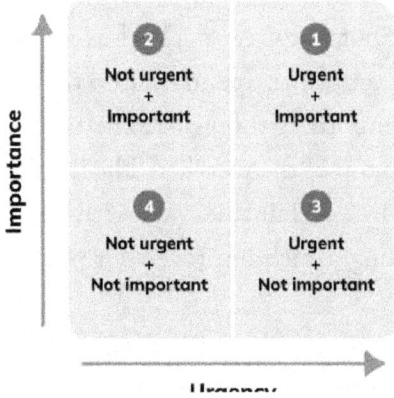

As you can see, the box has two axes: "urgency" on the horizontal axis and "importance" on the vertical axis. Each box in the grid represents a combination of those two values and all tasks can be placed in a box according to these guidelines.

Let's define the difference between urgent and important tasks. Urgent tasks need to be done immediately, such as replying to messages about a group project, putting out a house fire, attending to an urgent family matter, or providing emergency coverage for a shift at work. These things must be done within a specific time to maximize positive impacts or minimize negative impacts.

Important tasks are things that can contribute to your long-term success and could include things like obtaining a license, major family commitments, assignments, and internships. There is a significant impact associated with doing or not doing these things.

Let's put this all together.

Box 1 is urgent and important. These tasks are essential to your achieving success and reaching your goals. If they're not completed successfully or on time, there are serious negative impacts. These negative impacts could be anything from damaging trust in a relationship, to failing an assignment, or even losing your job! These tasks are likely to be high risk and high stress.

Box 2 is important but not urgent. This box should contain the tasks which will take most of your time. Spend time on them before they become urgent. Avoid letting important things become urgent (and stressful) by planning and getting on top of them earlier. The items in this box will help you achieve your goals in a sustainable way. Activities like exercise, eating healthy meals and relaxing, which improve your physical or mental health should fall into this box.

When you have important tasks with a deadline, wherever possible, you want to ensure you start working on them to give yourself time to get them done properly within the allotted time frame. This prevents them from becoming urgent and escalating into box 1 - bringing added stress with them.

Box 3 is urgent but not important. Tasks in this box do not contribute to your overall goals and you should be asking yourself why they are on your list. Consider whether they can be removed.

Box 4 is neither urgent nor important. Like box 3, tasks in box 4 don't contribute to your achieving important goals, nor is there any real motivation for you to work on them now. Again, you should limit the amount of time you spend on these tasks or eliminate them altogether.

Using the Eisenhower Matrix in your everyday life is a three-step process. It involves creating a list of tasks, mapping out those tasks onto the matrix, and assessing your priorities.

If you find you have too many items in box 1, consider the deadlines needed for each task, write them in your calendar, and ask yourself if they really belong in that box or if they can be added to box 2. Your goal is to try to eliminate or minimize everything in boxes 3 and 4. It might be a matter of telling someone no, and poof! They are gone.

This tool can help you to commit to your goals. Just remember to keep updating your lists and as time passes, so you can complete more tasks. That's the Eisenhower Matrix.

Next level of prioritization is up for discussion. Maybe you categorized your items perfectly using the Eisenhower Matrix and you've got a heap of things in box 1 and 2. But suddenly you feel a little nauseous thinking about all the stuff you must do. Don't sweat it. There is another proven method you can layer in to help you make those decisions.

The second method that can help you determine which activity to tackle first is the **80/20 Rule**, also known as the Pareto Principle. This rule states that you should focus 20% of your time on activities that will provide you with 80% of your results.

Here's how it works: If you have a list of 10 things to do, two of them will be far more valuable than the other eight items put together. Even if all

10 tasks take the same time to complete, those two items or the "vital few" will contribute to your goals far more than the "trivial many."

An example of this is trying to lose weight. You may come up with 19 things that will help you lose weight. But reducing calories and increasing daily exercise are going to be the two tasks that will help get you to an 80% success of your weight loss goal.

Regardless of your approach, make conscious efforts to prioritize your tasks and commit to your goals. Successful advocates, for themselves and others, learn to master these to defeat their distractions.

Distractions and Recovery from Setbacks

Ah, distractions. They are so sneaky and somewhat irresistible. They are also plentiful - social media, messenger, streaming TV, and any other non-productive activities. When you are advocating for human skills, tackling distractions can sometimes feel like trying to find a quiet space at a carnival.

One of the main reasons why it's so important to develop skills for managing distractions is that almost every device we use can be a source of distraction. We're fighting against an enemy that is built into the very tools we use to get things done and stay connected to others. And so it goes.

The only thing people can do is build up their defenses to deflect the distractions without breaking stride. It's useful to learn how to limit your access to them so you can remain focused.

Here are Seven Pro Tips to help you combat those tricky bastards and build up your distraction defenses:

Pro Tip #1: Give yourself a break. The human brain isn't designed to concentrate on high-intensity activities for hours on end. One way to ensure you take a break, but not fall into the trap of wasting time is to use a timer on your phone or smart watch. Aim for a 10 min break every 45-50 minutes.

This will allow for you to concentrate better than if you just worked straight through for many hours. Feel free to use that time for non-productive activities, but you need to be disciplined to ensure you return to your task once break time is over.

Pro Tip #2: Use built-in tools. Distraction is a common problem for everyone and most of our devices already have tools built in to help us deal with them. The "Do Not Disturb" feature on your phone is your friend. Use it during periods of time when you don't want any interruptions and then turn it off when you are done.

Most laptops have "focus assist" tools to minimize notifications unless they are urgent, or you can disable them completely for a time period. A lot of online messaging applications also can set your status so you can resist notifications when you don't want to receive them, and so other people can see that you are busy.

It's worth taking the time to learn about the tools you already have built into your devices and see how you can make them work towards managing distractions.

Pro Tip #3: Don't be afraid to ask for help. Don't forget it's okay to ask for the things you need to achieve your goals. That could mean you need to communicate with certain people to avoid disturbances during certain times. Most of us are fighting our own battle with distractions so if you communicate this need, most people will get it.

Pro Tip #4: Keep your goal in mind. Being clear on your end goal makes it easier to plan your activities towards achieving it. This helps you stay focused and reduces the likelihood you will become distracted. You can ask yourself, "Is this helping me achieve my goal?" when distractions come up and you need to get back on track.

Pro Tip #5: Set up a distraction-free environment. We have a colleague who laughs about a time when she was studying at her messy dorm desk with the door opened and a random man in the hallway leaned his head into her room and asked, "Do you want to go get waffles?" Instead of studying, she left with him, and as a result, did poorly on her exam.

Distraction-free environments could include having a dedicated space at home, free from televisions and other distractions. Or it could be about people. So, close your doors or hang a sign if you must avoid the delivery man, and stay away from too much clutter.

Pro Tip #6: Find your flow. Remember in the Honesty section when we learned about self-awareness and how you can use your strengths to shape your tasks? Your strengths can help surge you to be in a state of flow. That will make you less likely to be vulnerable to distractions.

Pro Tip #7: Keep practicing. The risk of not managing potential time wasters is that hours or sometimes days can go by without completing any tasks. This will only increase the pressure and stress you're already feeling once you realize you're not on track.

Don't be discouraged if you try but still find yourself falling victim to distractions. This happens to us all. If you find yourself in this situation, re-plan your priority tasks and reflect on what activities wasted your time and be conscious of limiting your exposure to them.

You can create anchors to help you, if you'd like. We know someone who has a post-it note on her television that says, "Are there more important things you could be doing?" She has this so she can avoid turning it on.

The more you practice, the more positive habits you will build that can help you quickly identify, manage, and recover from distractions. This can put an end to your time-wasting. You can do it!

And as you are trying to make an effective plan while building up your distraction defenses, oh fiddlesticks, a setback. These will happen and, at the time, they will suck. A setback is something, typically unexpected, that gets in the way of something you had planned or wanted to do. It often has a significant chance of impacting our ability to do something or causes us to change our plans.

But setbacks are also opportunities to get better and stronger. So, it pays to pick yourself up, dust yourself off, and get your ass back on track.

Not even the best laid plans are immune from setbacks because in many cases, we just don't see them coming. We want to achieve our goals but can't hide away from setbacks. We need to be able to learn, recover, and get back to our big picture goals.

The source of some setbacks might be directly in your control, like saying, "No," to unexpected plans, and others are not, such as the power going out in your apartment building. They can also be minor issues and things that slowly creep up on you or they can be major shocking events. It's important to understand the type of setback to work out how to best deal with them.

Problem setbacks slow you down or prevent you from doing something. For example, you may be working on a team project and someone in the team gets sick meaning you must re-organize your plans, so you don't miss the project deadline. Problems can also be things that creep up on you, such as having a lack of motivation.

Obstacle setbacks happen when there is a minor issue standing in your way, but it can be fixed easily. Examples include having to locate your laptop charger or having to attach a file to an email. These setbacks delay you and can be mildly frustrating.

Major setbacks occur when there is a serious and unexpected event that prevents you from obtaining your goal. This might include things such as a death of a relative, a terrible accident, or a major illness.

All setbacks, whatever type they are, need to be identified and dealt with to enable us to move forward and achieve our goals. Unless you can recover from setbacks, they will stop you from being able to do what you want. They can also impact your feelings and cause you to become stressed, angry, frustrated, and upset. Because you can't control everything, setbacks WILL occur. So how can people deal with them?

Well first off, it's important to be proactive. If you fail to respond to setbacks, they are harder to recover from and can get even worse. For example, imagine you're having a low-motivation week. Then it continues for a month and then a year.

As time goes on, you fail to address the issue and naturally, you slip further and further behind in achieving the things you want in life. This obviously will take a toll on you emotionally. In this case, a minor problem that could have been rectified with a correction upfront could eventually become a major setback. For each setback type, approach it as if doing nothing is not an option, knowing major consequences could be the result of your inaction.

Remind yourself that even if it's a major issue, think of it as a setback, not the end of the world. You can rationally think through the actions that you need to take to recover. You can recover and might even come out of the situation in a better position than when you started.

Setbacks help us grow. They can make us more resilient and even more successful. We just need to know how to face them. The more you face setbacks head on, the easier it will become to rebound and bounce back better than ever.

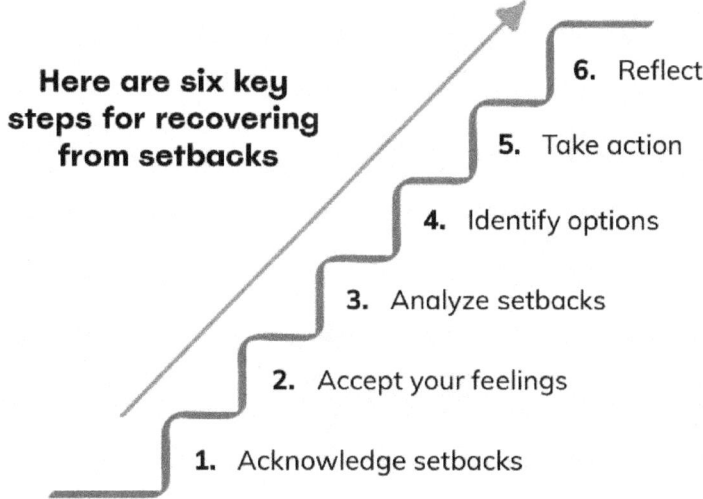

Here are six key steps for recovering from setbacks

1. Acknowledge setbacks
2. Accept your feelings
3. Analyze setbacks
4. Identify options
5. Take action
6. Reflect

Step #1: Acknowledge setbacks. Identify them and acknowledge that a setback has occurred. If you ignore it, it won't go away, and you may fail to take action allowing you to move forward.

While major setbacks may seem obvious, the smaller problems may not be. To identify potential setbacks, periodically track your progress on your goals, on projects at work, and so on. When your progress lags, look for causes, for example, if you're lagging on a work project that correlates with regularly being late to work. But you recognize being late stems from being too tired. Your setback is, in this case, lack of sleep.

Step #2: Accept your feelings. When a setback occurs, you can experience a range of different feelings. It's okay and normal to feel disappointed, angry, upset, and/or hurt. As hard as it is, you have to acknowledge and accept these emotions when faced with setbacks, even though you may be tempted to avoid them. Once you give yourself permission to accept your feelings it is easier to move past them so you can work on what you need to do.

Step #3: Analyze setbacks. With some setbacks, there is simply nothing you could have done to change it and you need to accept that. Other times there may have been things in our control that could have changed the outcome. Either way, take a step back and objectively observe what happened. Think about the circumstances of the setback, not just from your point of view but that of others.

Setbacks are events that give us important information. You should gain as much insight as you can so, if possible, you can avoid the setback happening again. Or if you experience another setback in the future, you can be better equipped to deal with it. Try to imagine it happening to someone else. Talk to others. Remain open to what others say. Ask if it's happened before.

Step #4: Identify options. When a setback happens, that means there has been a change to your plans or that the reality of your situation hasn't matched your expectations. You need to work out what options you have now that the circumstances have changed. You should aim to generate a few different options to enable yourself to choose the best one. If it helps, consult with others.

A setback can't be changed. It's already happened. *What do you do next?* Well, you always have options.

After a setback our choices become: (a) do nothing, (b) try again or persevere without changing what or how you tackle the problem, or (c) do something differently.

Spoiler alert! Chances are options (a) and (b) will not work and you will get frustrated by experiencing the same setback over and over again.

So instead, try something different. If you think creatively enough, you can generate some good options that will enable you to still achieve your goals.

To generate these ideas, it can be helpful to discuss it with others and/or ask yourself a few questions to get you thinking such as:

What can/can't change?
Only focus on the things within your control. There is no value trying to change something you have no control over.

Do you want to change?
This may be something to consider if you think you may need to change who you are or compromise your own personal values.

What is involved in making the change?
Of the things you can change, what do you need to do to make the change? When one thing changes, often there are flow-on impacts to other aspects in your life.

How much risk are you prepared to take?
Different options will come with different levels of certainty and risk. It's best to understand these to help decide the right option for you.

Have your goals changed?
After a setback, it is a good opportunity to think about your goals and make sure you still want to achieve the things you set out to do. Goals sometimes do change, and that's okay. But you will want to know when that's happened so you can re-orientate to the right path.

Asking yourself these questions will enable you to narrow down what options are genuinely available and realistic for you. This way you can get back on the horse and get going again.

Step #5: Take action. Now that you've decided on an option to respond to the setback, you can create a plan to act and move forward. Soon your setback will be behind you. Take the time to plan properly so you can give yourself confidence in your actions. Be kind to yourself. Everyone makes mistakes.

Bad things happen. In the kindest way possible, get over it, and don't dwell on the setback. Learn from the experience and remember that you can only take action on things you can control.

Step #6: Reflect. Setbacks are the gift that keeps on giving in terms of your learning and growth. They give you the opportunity to respond when they happen and the chance to reflect on your response.

After responding to setbacks, take some time to reflect on how you recovered. Consider what worked and what you'd like to do differently next time.

Let's put all these steps together by looking at a circumstance of how someone might go through them. We know you've been waiting for more human examples, so without further ado, meet Lydia.

Lydia was unsuccessful in getting a promotion she wanted at work and was very upset about this. For Lydia, this is a major setback.

Acknowledge and Accept: The acknowledgement part is easy here. She wanted a promotion and thought she was going to get it, but she didn't. She knows she didn't get something she was hoping to achieve.

She is experiencing feelings of anger, but she knows she needs to accept those feelings to move past them and begin to look at things objectively to move forward.

Analyze: She asks herself some probing questions to understand more fully what's really getting in the way of her achieving her goals:

Why did I want that promotion? Because it would make me feel valued. *Why is it important to me that I feel valued?* Because I'm the middle child at home in a large family and I have always felt ignored.

In this case, Lydia's goal was not in fact getting that promotion, but instead it is to feel recognized and not ignored. This process has allowed her to broaden her thinking to open-up more (and better) options to recover from the setback.

Explore options: Lydia might come up with a few ideas after having talked to a colleague. One of these might be joining a committee at work. This will allow her to contribute her ideas in a more meaningful and impactful way. This will help her achieve her true goal of feeling valued. Joining the committee is something that is entirely within her control and will help her achieve her goal. Tick, tick!

Take action and Reflect: Now, having her plan in mind, Lydia reaches out to the head of the committee and asks about how she can get involved. Ironically, focusing on achieving her core goal and being less fixated on this promotion makes Lydia much less stressed at work and much nicer to work with. She even gets that next promotion!

Thinking back, she realizes how important it is to her to be working alongside other people who are working towards a common goal, and she focuses on doing this as much as she can in her job to feel more fulfilled. The promotion was an added bonus.

Lydia was successful because she was an advocate of her own value. Someone who is an advocate of human skills contributes value by instilling in themselves and others the belief that they can succeed in work and in life. Advocates practice the skills needed for growth such as mindfulness, owning their behaviors, and reflection. Be like Lydia.

As a human skills advocate, you can plant the seed that will contribute so much value to the world. When you recognize mindfulness and seek the quest for balance, you can become the person who makes a difference.

When you are a resilient, kind, grateful, and growth- minded person, you can influence the actions of others. And through your observations, you can make your actions more effective.

Remember not to give into distractions and that recovery from your setbacks is possible. You can be an advocate that will set and commit to your goals with focused intention. As a result, the world will become a better place because of your human skills. And now that you've had a chance to learn these human skills you can then advocate for others.

Successful Humans Advocate for Practicing Human Skills

"If your life is cloudy and you're far, far off course, you may have to go on faith for a while, but eventually you'll learn that every time you trust your internal navigation system, you end up closer to your right life."
–Martha Beck[lxviii]

Part Five

"N"

<u>Navigate</u> a Creative Pathway to Success

NAVIGATE

For centuries, kings and queens would call upon brave navigators to imagine the possibilities of exploring the world. They were curious, creative, and innovative enough to turn their fantasies into reality. With persistence, they unleashed their potential and contributed to something greater than themselves.

If you want to obtain success, you'll need to participate in an adventure that consists of exciting and unusual experiences. You also need to understand how to be a navigator.

A navigator studies the process of monitoring and controlling the movement of a craft from one place to another. Although complex in its execution, it is their job to create a roadmap to a specific location. In simple terms, a navigator can answer two basic questions: Where am I? And where am I going? Without this knowledge it is nearly impossible to determine if they are moving forward in the right direction.

Imagine if people could become navigators who could precisely answer these questions about their lives. Do you know where you are?

Where are you going? Can you envision it on the horizon? If not the actual place, the direction? Your goals may point you there, but can you forge your own path, a creative path to go somewhere amazing?

If success is your ultimate destination, self-doubt and worry will then be a thing of the past. Dare we say there is a way.

How? You must become a navigator who can forge the creative path as you venture into the unknown.

Let Curiosity Fuel You

"Why?" is the question a curious person regularly asks themselves before they begin to navigate the pathway to success. It is the fuel of their emotional reactions to everything they create and everything that happens to them.

Imagine how quickly your confusion sets in as you bite into a grape that tastes like delicious cotton candy. Once you give into your curiosity, you realized the cause was due to crossbreeding of many different standard grapes. Then your confusion turns into being pleasantly surprised. While this is a random example, it illustrates the importance of seeking to understand the truth behind things as you see them. As a result, you are more likely to accept the situation if you can explain the reason underneath the surface.

When a little kid asks "Why?" and then you answer them, and then they ask "Why?" again and again, it can be annoying. But kids are so great at stopping at nothing until they better understand. Their curious minds want to drill down to the cause and effect for everything so they can make meaning of things and learn about the world.

As you grow into an adult, your curiosity is stifled, or it diminishes. It does this because you stop asking questions out of fear, doubt, and worry of not fitting in.

Some adults might assume what they believe or know is right when the unknown seems scary. They even create boundaries to remain safe and they resist change since they think staying fixed in one place is easier. Eventually, they decide that taking the well-worn path is easier. Stop this.

You must remember that curious questions have the power to stimulate, provoke, inform, and inspire! Every year sees so many new ideas emerge to grab our attention. Our needs and wants change constantly and we rely on curious people to keep us moving forward. Choosing to navigate this pathway will open up new vistas.

There are certain characteristics of curious thinkers. They don't think they are trapped within the confines of what seems comfortable and typical.

Curious people ask questions such as:

How can we make it better?

What else can we do?

What if?

Curiosity is expressed by an inquisitive mind that asks questions and has an ability to think differently. The courage to take risks and persevere are the two most important characteristics of a curious person.

Not only did curiosity make Carl Benz[lxix] one of the world's greatest inventors, it is also the top trait employers look for when making hiring decisions. This is because it indicates an ability to learn, contribute, and improve current affairs.

Curiosity is a skill people are born with. The problem is, we train ourselves to stifle it as we get older. But trust us. The power of curiosity is already within you. It is just going to take some work to navigate the path to unleash it. **To get started, here are three ways you can unleash your curiosity.**

Way #1: Ask more questions. Being inquisitive is a choice. You can either pretend to know something or you can ask, "Why?" to dig beneath what seems obvious. Never be ashamed to ask questions even when those around you just want you to shut up so everyone can move on. It's a balance.

Don't ask a question for the sake of asking a question. And you probably shouldn't ask a question that can be answered easily at another time. However, it is a good idea to ask a question if something doesn't feel quite right to you.

Way #2: Reconnect with your inner child. Are you willing to be a little ridiculous? Try to find your lost sense of wonder and take nothing for granted. Think about and explain things from a child's perspective. Find activities that will stimulate your creativity.

Bring on the Lego© sets, crayons, and scented markers! Explore your ideas by scribbling down keywords, drawing fantastical images, and telling epic picture stories. Break out the stick people if you must, but either way, try hard to ignore the real-world rules of your imagination.

This approach will allow you to see all the places, events, people, and ideas you come across day to day with a new sense of discovery. This step will allow you to be the type of person who thinks through the eyes of someone who is learning things for the very first time.

Way #3: Be a unicorn. Stretch yourself to expand your current experience, even if you feel uncomfortable. Keep asking yourself, "What's the worst that can happen?"

Ironically, it is only when we become adults that our brains are developed enough to process new discoveries and turn them into concrete ideas and strategies. Take Erin, for example. She tasted cotton candy grapes and became curious about crossbreeding fruits. This led her to ask more questions and embrace her inner child. Eventually, she became a unicorn by thinking about different creative approaches to cross-pollinate familiar fruits. This is how she discovered she has the potential to introduce and sell new species of fruits at her farmer's market. So really, if we don't try to re-develop curiosity, we are wasting our own potential to bring our creative ideas to life.

Drive Your Creativity

Creativity is the ability to use your big old brain's imagination to bring your original ideas to life! This process can happen like a flash of insight otherwise known as having a "light bulb" moment or it can happen more slowly. Either way, it is an act of turning new ideas into reality.

Your workplace creative path begins with the knowledge that it is mission critical for businesses to keep up with rapidly evolving customer expectations and to stay ahead of the competition. Creative people who can step in and help solve complex problems will be very valuable to employers and society alike. This is because creativity helps us find ways to live longer, be more connected, and lead productive lives. Being curious, asking questions, opens up our minds to being or becoming this kind of creative person.

People who use creativity can perceive and interpret the complex world around them. With it, they can make valuable contributions and get out of hard moments. It is a critical skill that contributes to their ability to navigate the problem-solving process. As a result, they achieve great things. But creativity, valuable as it is, doesn't happen automatically, especially as we become adults.

In 1968, researcher George Land conducted a study of 1,600 children between the ages of three and five years old. He used the same creativity test he developed to select the most innovative engineers and scientists that work for NASA. He tested the same children at 10 years of age and again at 15 years of age.

The results of his research were fascinating. In children three to five years old, it was reported that 98% were creative and imaginative. With children that were 10 years old, that dropped to 30% and only 12% of 15-year-olds were reported to be creative. Here is the shocking part. When the same test was given to 280,000 adults, the creativity rate was just 2%![lxx]

The study revealed that we are all born naturally creative, and as we grow older, our instinct to explore is tempered by our desire to conform to society. We stop asking questions because we learn that it might make us look silly. We stop being open to uncertainty and vulnerability because we are worried about making mistakes. In other words, just like with curiosity, we stifle our own creativity, out of fear.

You should not be fearful of trying to rekindle your stale relationship with creativity. People can learn to be creative by experimenting, exploring, questioning assumptions, using imagination, and synthesizing information.

Many people think creativity is a gift. You either have it or you don't. This is simply not true. Anyone can develop it, and there are processes you can adopt to support creativity in problem solving. It takes practice and a willingness to step beyond your comfort zone.

There are four practical steps to get you started navigating your creativity journey.

Step #1: Start with a positive attitude. If you want to be more creative, you must cultivate a positive attitude. Positive thinking releases dopamine in our brains. This chemical increase feelings of happiness, and it is responsible for our creativity.

Tina Seeling, author of *inGenius* suggests that, "In order to find creative solutions to big problems, you must first believe that you'll find them. With this attitude, you see opportunities where others see obstacles and are able to leverage the resources you have to reach your goals." So basically, positivity unlocks our energy reserves and opens our minds to push our thinking further.[lxxi]

Step #2: Find and remove what gets in the way of your creative mind. Begin by asking yourself reflective questions such as:

Are you humble enough to continuously learn from others and the world?

Are you confident enough to be vulnerable, to be wrong for the sake of learning something new?

Can you suspend the need to be right for the sake of ego and appearance?

Do you feel able to challenge your own thinking that you already know or have the answer to something?

Can you choose new experiences over uncertainty?

Are you hopeful and excited about exploration over the fear of failure or the unknown?

Are you letting the attention of others determine your creative success?

Spend some time reflecting on these questions. You might consider thinking about what your existing views and opinions might be and ask yourself if they are getting in the way of you considering new points of view.

Joseph Gordon-Levitt claims it is better to pay attention (another way to say be in the flow) than to get attention when it comes to creativity. In a TED Talk on August 20th, 2019, he said, "I think that our creativity is becoming more and more of a means to an end, and that end is to get attention."[lxxii]

He felt compelled to speak up because his experience of getting attention had a negative impact on his creative process. As a result, he felt unfulfilled and unhappy. Like him, people need to think about ways they can try to break down their barriers and recognize when they are getting in the way of their own creative process.

Step #3: Open your mind. Say, "Yes," to new opportunities. Daydream. Even if you have to plan time to do it and it feels forced at first. Encourage yourself to explore your thoughts and welcome the unexpected without freaking out. Try to see the unpredictable as a way of learning new and wonderful things about yourself.

Do this and you will become a keen observer and learner rather than a person who lets things pass you by without even noticing.

Step #4: Find other inquisitive minds. Speak to people you wouldn't normally speak to and really listen to what they have to say, even if you don't agree with their perspective. When interacting with people who are different from you, be interested in who they are, and try to learn something from them through their expressions, backgrounds, and suggestions.

People experience creativity in different ways. Sometimes it happens just by perceiving the world in new ways or by generating new solutions to old problems. It can also happen by making connections between seemingly unrelated facts or events.

Successful people navigate a creative path to explore possibilities. They are "outside of the box" or lateral thinkers who generate passion and excitement! They also look at things from different perspectives and find answers that are not immediately apparent. This will open your mind to innovative new ideas and solutions.

Steer Towards Innovation

Innovation is the producing component of creativity. It drives the introduction of something new. This could be a new idea, new imagination, or new inventions. It produces an output that people can engage with, understand, and see value in.

Innovators change things. They take new ideas, sometimes their own, sometimes other people's, and then they develop them. This development involves promoting those ideas until they become an accepted part of daily life.

Innovation requires self-confidence and the guts to take risks. It also requires the willingness to fail and learn with a vision of what the future might bring. People who navigate a creative path to success have all these characteristics, but it can take them many years to develop them fully.

Steve Jobs[lxxiii] and his team had innovative traits when they launched the iPhone. They repurposed software and technology from other products available in the market then re-imagined their uses to create the concept of a handheld computer that could make phone calls, play music, and browse the internet.

Innovation doesn't exclusively deliver positive outcomes that lead to multi-billion-dollar ideas, but overall, it moves us in a positive direction. There is absolutely no substitution for being able to think creatively as a contributor to innovative ideas. This will indeed help you with your accomplishments if it is your intention to thrive.

This idea of being an innovative thinker is old school and history proves it. Get this: back in 1666, Sir Isaac Newton, one of the most influential scientists in history, was under an apple tree when he saw an apple fall to the ground.[lxxiv]

He pondered why the apple fell downward not sideways or upward. He could have looked at that apple and accepted the status quo that apples can only fall downwards. He could have just moved on with his life. Luckily for the many who have benefited from his theory since, he didn't accept things just because of his current experiences. He remained curious and wanted to learn more.

This event sparked a moment of creative inspiration that led to Newton developing his concept of gravity. Life changing, world changing. This story became one of the most iconic examples of the creative moment, and it cements the fact that society has historically needed innovative thinkers.

Speaking of history, imagine a world before personal computers, the internet, and smartphones. Some of us have lived it. In the mid to late 80s, technology became commonly used in the workplace and households. The internet began its mainstream adoption about a decade later in the 90s and smartphones took off in the early 2000s. These ground-breaking innovations all started with curiosity, which led to being creative, and ultimately, an innovative idea was born.

These inventions may seem like fundamental parts of your reality, but we all know they didn't always exist. New realities are constantly emerging, and innovative minds are the inventors. They are also the architects of the world's new realities because they are comfortable exploring the possibilities of the world as people know it.

But these innovative minds are not wizards who just magically navigated the creative path. Innovation is not just a skill that comes to them out of thin air.

They are human beings using their innovation skills to challenge their current reality. They engage in innovative processes to navigate through new and better ways of doing things.

To become an innovator, thinking and acting creatively is the key to shaping your future. This way of thinking relies on something called productive reasoning or the ability to combine curiosity, creativity, and innovation with critical thinking.

Adam Kahane in *Solving Tough Problems* articulates this approach perfectly when describing the Mont Fleur Team. They were trying to solve problems of post-apartheid South Africa. "When they listened, they were not just reloading their old tapes. They were receptive to new ideas. More than that, they were willing to be influenced and changed. They held their ideas lightly; they noticed and questioned their own thinking; they separated themselves from their ideas. ('I am not my ideas, and so you and I can reject them without rejecting me.') They 'suspended' their ideas, as if on strings from the ceiling, and walked around and looked at these ideas from different perspectives."[lxxv]

Planning for a post-apartheid South Africa, the period after the end of segregation or discrimination based on race, was something no one had ever done. There was no playbook or manual on how to plan for this world. It relied on this group of people to step into the unknown and do the best they could together with a purpose. There were no wrong answers, there were no right answers, just a whole lot of unanswered questions to be tackled and a future full of potential to be shaped.

When navigating through the unknown, we want you to know there are **six strategic ways you can unlock your potential and learn to innovate.**

Way #1: Associate by connecting the dots. Knowledge alone is not useful unless you can make connections between what you know. Keep in mind that you are constantly building on what came before. Within every new possibility there will be some prior knowledge of something already solved, either by you or someone else.

That's why it also helps to ask yourself who else has faced this problem. When you seek out and adapt solutions or approaches from other places or thought leaders, you might discover surprising new possibilities.

Way #2: Ask questions. The most successful innovators know how to ask tough questions that challenge the assumptions of others. They are not only prone to asking, "Why, how, what if, and why not?" they also tend to play the devil's advocate by pushing themselves to embrace seemingly opposing ideas. They impose hypothetical constraints to force themselves to think outside the box.

Way #3: Pay attention. Innovators have mastered the habit of observing what is going on around them- the way they or other people behave, interact, and react. They notice seemingly unimportant details that give them great insight into how to significantly improve how something works, how it can evolve, and what its purpose is.

Way #4: Experiment. For innovators, the world is their laboratory. They are constantly trying out new ideas and creating prototypes that can be put into action. They test things, and they learn from their experiments. The good ideas they keep and the ones that didn't work, they either store for further analysis or they get rid of them. Then they start all over again. They use a cycle where they plan, act, and adjust. They do this over and over again until they perfect their ideas.

Way #5: Collaborate. The most innovative entrepreneurs are those who have made networking part of their routine. They go out of their way to meet diverse people from all walks of life who are intentionally different from them. This presents radically different perspectives. This constant, sometimes counterintuitive, networking allows them to make unexpected connections between concepts and can provide them with some of their most valuable insights.

Way #6: Delay judgement. Often great ideas start as crazy ones. If judgement and critique are applied too early, an idea will be killed and never developed into something useful and usable. This doesn't mean there is never a time for critique in the creative process but knowing the right time to apply it is essential to achieving the desired outcome. Many new ideas, because they are unfamiliar, seem strange, silly, ridiculous, and far-fetched.

Only later do they become amazing ideas that everyone wished they had thought of. Some ideas, when originally developed, may be too crazy to do anything with but in the hands of the right thinkers they will become potentially game changing products or services. Critical to making this happen is the ability to suspend judgement, remain optimistic, and adapt when disruptions happen.

Adapt the Disruptive Fog

Adaptability is your ally in this chaotic and complex world. In general, your adaptability to the unknown will shape your capacity to anticipate the issues that will influence your future actions. If you are adaptable, not only can you understand the consequences of these issues and actions, but you can also navigate through challenges by finding creative solutions.

Eventually you can learn to appreciate the interdependence of variables and they can help you interpret and address relevant opportunities. Being adaptable will help you forge a path towards success in a world of constant disruption.

Disruption is everywhere. Businesses are continually using disruptive business models and technologies because they think they can make a lot of money by taking a new approach to traditional ways of providing products and services. Sometimes they are right as this model aims to meet people's needs in newer and better ways that break the mold of what's currently being done. They use disruption to take advantage of the latest trends, and then they push those trends to create more opportunities.

Successful businesses adapt to change and force their competitors to adapt as well. In today's world, the pace of disruption is rapidly increasing, and it's not going to stop anytime soon. You are either disrupting or being disrupted. There is no in between.

The retail industry gets it. Anyone heard of the online marketplace Amazon? They practically assaulted the world of retail by forcing department stores, who have not embraced digital transformation, to vanish from the market.

How did they do this? By adapting and disrupting the retail market. Then Amazon used their creativity skills to navigate a new business model of low price, fast delivery, and a wide selection of products.

The transportation industry gets it too. Remember that ride sharing service Uber coming to town? This was the taxi-driver's worst nightmare as this competition virtually eliminated them from the market. Like it or not, Uber's future growth strategy is to disrupt and take business away from delivery companies and courier services. They did this by creatively adapting how users can navigate through the process of booking a car and driver.

Tourism has seen its share of disruption as well. Airbnb is overrunning the hotel industry, paying no tax to local authorities, and hurting the residential property market in popular cities. But like it or not, they found a creative approach to adapt to how people navigate the process of planning vacations in a changing world.

Then there are the companies that went from market dominance to obscurity in a blink of an eye due to disruption and their failure to navigate the changing market around them. Rest in peace Myspace, Kodak, Blockbuster, Pan-Am, and Blackberry, just to name a few.

Don't even get us started on higher education! Colleges face a combination of challenges such as economic crises and globalism. Not to mention the emerging technologies that are daunting to learn and intimidating to implement. Then there is navigating a path of success through the crippling debt and, of course, the degrees that can't guarantee job placement. We could go on, but we will spare you the rant.

The big takeaway here is that the world's growing disruption, complexity, and diversity present both challenge and opportunity. Take globalism for example. On one hand, globalism can contribute to economic inequality, social division, and conflict. On the other hand, if navigated correctly, it can bring important new perspectives, innovation, and improved living standards.

Technology is another example. On one hand it distracts us, is expensive, and has created a lack of privacy. On the other hand, it helps us shop, begin relationships, and makes research a simple process.

Disruption. Rapid change. Uncertainty. The Unknown. These words and others describe the challenges we face in this world. One term has emerged to describe the nature of these challenges and that term is **VUCA.**[lxxvi]

This term is an acronym which stands for **Volatile, Uncertain, Complex, and Ambiguous.** *That sounds pretty heavy, huh?*

The thing is it doesn't have to be. What we should be doing is flipping and changing our attitude towards these challenges when we can so disruptions can be used to our advantage.

If you recognize a disruption as a new normal, you can use it to your advantage. As you are trying to navigate a path to success, take a creative approach, and see what happens. For instance, instead of fighting in vain against the VUCA world, you can embrace it.

Take Clorox for example. This is the new normal: "Fiscal year 2021 was an extraordinary year for Clorox, with the pandemic putting us through the test of volatility, including rapid changes in consumer demand and inflationary pressure, which is reflected in our fourth quarter results," said CEO Linda Rendle.

This is the company demonstrating their resilience: "It reinforced the strength of our global portfolio, which has never been more relevant to consumers. And it showed the opportunity to accelerate our IGNITE strategy to capitalize on changing consumer trends, differentiate Clorox and win in our categories."[lxxvii]

The volatility, complexity, uncertainty, and ambiguity feelings you might have can lessen over time by navigating in an adaptive way.

Consider the following four thinking strategies as you forge your path towards success:

Strategy #1: Counter volatility with vision. Create change by adapting your vision so you are clear about your values. They will guide you to consider the kind of future you want. Knowing your values helps you accept and embrace change as a constant, unpredictable feature in your personal and work environments. Don't resist it.

Vision can happen in times of volatility as change offers great opportunity. Successful people know that as things change, their approach needs to evolve as well.

Strategy #2: Meet uncertainty with understanding. Create moments to help you understand and develop new ways of thinking. Pause to listen, look around, observe, and reflect. You can then think of creative ways to act in response to uncertain elements.

Take this time to review and evaluate yourself. *What are you doing well? What came as a surprise? What could you do differently next time?* Simulate and experiment with ideas and situations.

Strategy #3: React to complexity with clarity. Communicate clearly with people around you. Express your creativity by sharing your ideas with other people in a way they can easily understand. Some challenging situations can get even more complicated when you and those around you are not on the same page about change.

Strategy #4: Fight ambiguity with agility. Promote flexibility and adaptability. Plan, but build in time for the unexpected and be prepared to alter your plans if/as required. Practice dealing with change using your creative thinking skills. Get comfortable with adaptation rather than fight it. Keep asking, "What's the worst that could happen?"

Unfortunately, even if navigators use these adaptation strategies, they can't know everything that will happen in the future. But they can create an environment that can help them approach decision-making and problem solving in a creative way.

Push Your Environment to the Metal

If you Google a picture of Einstein's desk, you'll see that there is a history of creative minds thriving in disorganized environments. Some people use this as an excuse to have a desk that looks like it threw up paperwork and got attacked by sticky notes. We are not here to judge you or them. All we are saying is, if you're trying to navigate a creative pathway to success it helps if you create an environment that enables you to be more productive.

A creative environment is a setting that encourages you to partake in innovation. It's a place that allow you to have the freedom to introduce new ways to approach your work. In its physical form, when you are there, you feel comfortable and inspired.

One of the elements of a creative working environment is it includes spaces that allow you to be self-sufficient when creating projects. These spaces should be appropriate in size so you can perform your duties in ways you deem fit. If you are part of a team, everyone should feel free enough to explore multiple spaces depending on their needs.

The spaces of your creative working environment should be filled with another element, resources. More specifically, resources that are helpful since they allow you to perform your job more efficiently. These may include tangible things like office supplies or intangible things such as a designated budget that can eventually help you troubleshoot your future challenges.

But what if you're trying to navigate a creative space and you have a starving artist budget? No problem. There are loads of ways you can create an environment when your funds are low. One of our favorite ways it to buy green screen fabric and hang it on a clothesline (less than 15 dollars) rather than buying a green screen (a few hundred dollars). If you'd like a list with more ideas, feel free to email us directly via hello@successishuman.com.

As an added bonus, regardless of budget, the spaces in your creative working environment can and should be customized to suit your personality. But as a word of caution, this should be decided with consideration to how you work best. Let's take our friend Ursula so you can see what we mean.

Ursula likes the color purple. She also likes cats. Her coworkers know this about her, and every time it's her birthday, Mother's Day, or a holiday, they give Ursula gifts that incorporate the things she likes.

Now Ursula is sitting in a purple room adorned by purple supplies. What's worse is she is completely surrounded by figurines and posters of cats. Yikes. It has become really hard for her to concentrate.

You see the problem? Customization to the extreme affects your ability to concentrate, and ultimately it will affect your ability to be creative. Instead, Ursula could incorporate just a few personal items that bring her joy and, even better, inspire her to feel more comfortable so she can be more creative.

Creative spaces can happen digitally too. If done correctly, they can lead to more productivity. Take Ursula's *digital dashboard* for example.

This space is made digitally using spreadsheets and it helps Ursula navigate her daily links. Ursula likes using it since she tends to accidentally close her browser. This way, she only has to open one file. It also allows Ursula to minimize the amount of tabs she has opened.

To be successful, we need to push the pedal to the metal and navigate our spaces and resources in creative ways. A productive environment will help your mind produce a higher quality of work. And you'll need all the help you can get, especially since our minds sometimes default to our existing perspectives and biases when we get into a questionable situation.

Shift Your Thinking

To be creative, you need to navigate in a way such that you see things from different perspectives. In times like these, it helps to know that your thinking will sometimes revert to your existing perspectives and biases when you need to make decisions. This is something to keep in mind before we talk about thinking caps.

Your mind filters information. This happens a lot because our brains constantly need to process a huge amount of information very quickly. Since we can't process everything, we need to find shortcuts to cope. In fact, our lifestyle often exposes us to about 11 million pieces of information at any given time. We can only process about 40. That's 0.00036%![lxxviii]

It makes sense. Our mind attempts to avoid information overload by applying filters using something called the *ladder of inference*.

This is a concept that was developed by psychologist Chris Argyris and later applied by Peter Senge in the book *The Fifth Discipline*. Basically, your brain takes snapshots of data all around you, almost like photos that are stored in your brain. Then you assess the photos, but immediately your brain takes shortcuts by applying filters to this new information to process it as quickly as possible.[lxxix]

When you have applied your filter to the "photo" you will infer personal meaning from what you see and form assumptions. Those assumptions will allow you to draw conclusions which can lead to strong beliefs. Finally, those beliefs lead to decisions and actions. So, the ladder in your brain sort of looks like this:

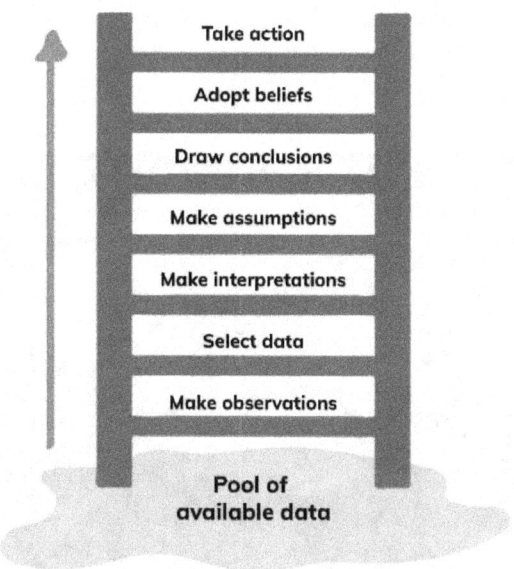

The problem is, these timesaving filters are based on existing beliefs, which are based on past experiences and opinions. In other words, our existing beliefs influence our new observations. This is known as a "reflective loop." And this filter can blind you to new perspectives regarding new information. You will basically see what you want to see regardless of what else the new information might be saying.

The Rubin Vase is an example of how our brains apply these filters to new information based on our perspectives.[lxxx]

If you perceive the black image is the important part of this picture, then you will undoubtedly see a black vase. If you perceive the white part of this picture is more important, then you'll probably spot the two opposing faces first.

But some of these images are more challenging. Try this one on for size:

Did you perceive a young girl or an old woman?[lxxxi]

For challenging times, with awareness of filters, successful people navigate a pathway by putting on their thinking caps - thank goodness! This creative approach allows them to consider different perspectives to find solutions.

The concept of putting on your thinking cap or hat is not new. It has been used in one form or another since the 17th century to indicate that sometimes you have to think hard if you are trying to solve a problem.

This idea has been incorporated into one of the top brainstorming techniques known as **The Six Thinking Hats.** In 1985, physician, author, and consultant, Edward de Bono developed this method to teach thinking as a subject in schools.[lxxxii]

He hoped this would later be used by students in business and in life. It's a strategy that teaches students to be flexible thinkers by identifying six different ways or styles of thinking, each representing a colored "thinking hat." The concept is, as you wear each hat, you learn how to think in different ways (see image below) so you can brainstorm and approach problems from various angles.

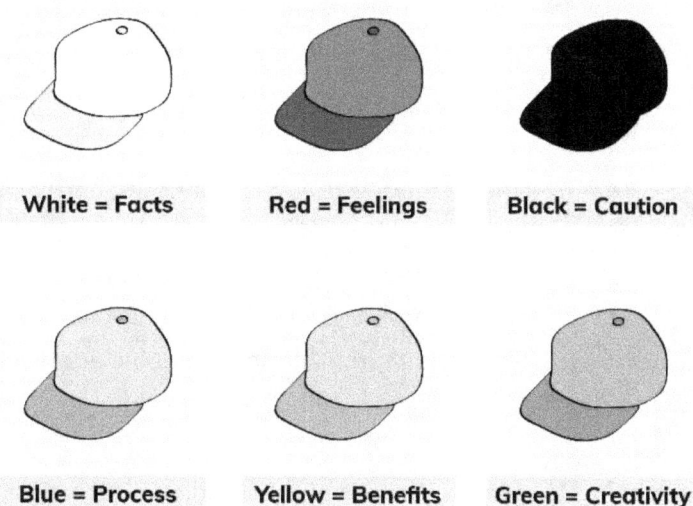

This creative method helps you broaden your approach to decision-making and problem solving. It is effective because often the best decisions come from changing the way you think about problems and examining them from different viewpoints. It forces you to move outside your normal way of thinking, which can be difficult to do, especially if you are under pressure.

Nobody understands pressure better than everyone's favorite hobbit, Frodo Baggins from *The Fellowship of the Ring*. In case you've never heard of him, he is the protagonist from author's J. R. R. Tolkien's writings, and he has to undertake the quest to destroy an evil ring by tossing it into the fires of a place called Mount Doom. His problem? It's all the way in this wicked place called Mordor, and Fordo has never left the comforts of Shire, his hometown. Regardless, as he approaches this problem, Frodo will try on the six hats.

Wearing the White Hat (facts) helps Frodo focus on available facts and data. This allows him to look at the information that he has, analyze past trends, and see what he can learn from it. It also allows him to look for gaps in his knowledge and try to either fill them in or take account of them.

With this white hat, he can gather information using problem solving questions such as "What do or don't you know about the issue? What can you learn from this situation? What information do you need to solve the problem? Are there potential existing solutions that you can use to solve the problem?"

With the white hat on, Frodo navigates a creative path when he learns that destroying the ring will involve traveling on a treacherous journey, but it is one he must endure if he wants to save the home he loves. He also learns that the ring is very powerful, and he probably should avoid putting it on. As he embarks on this quest, a potential solution might include being willing to accept the help of the other people who accompany him.

Wearing the Red Hat (feelings) will help Frodo look at problems using his intuition, gut reaction, and emotions. In use, he will not only think about his own emotions but also how others could react emotionally. This will enable him to try to understand the responses of people who do not fully know his reasoning. When he gathers information from his emotions, he should be able to intuitively relate these feelings to the problems he is trying to solve.

With this red hat on, Frodo asks himself: "What's your gut feeling about this solution? Based on feelings, is there another way to fix the problem? Does your intuition tell you your chosen solution is the right one?"

This red hat allows Frodo to navigate a creative path by thinking about his internal struggle with self-doubt about his quest. Although he and his team are full of trepidation, his intuition of knowing the value of their home outweighs his reluctance. Therefore, his solution must be to set off on the arduous journey that lies ahead.

Wearing the Black Hat (caution) helps Frodo look at a decision's potentially negative outcomes. With this mindset, he can look at the situation cautiously and defensively as he tries to see what might not work. This is important because it highlights the weak points in a plan. It allows him to eliminate them, alter them, or prepare contingency plans to counter them.

Black hat thinking helps Frodo make his plans "tougher" and more resilient. It can also help him spot fatal flaws and risks before he embarks on a plan of action.

The black hat provides one of the real benefits of this model since many successful people get used to thinking positively and don't see the problems in advance. This leaves them under-prepared as they cannot anticipate difficulties.

Adorned with his black hat, Frodo navigates a creative path by asking himself questions such as: "How will this idea likely fail? What is the fatal flaw in this plan? What are the potential risks and consequences? Do we have the resources, skills, and ability to make this work?"

As Frodo discovers, there are indeed many potential risks on his journey, such as having to face many deadly enemies, from malicious goblins and orcs to flying fellbeasts and evil wizards. Yikes! In anticipation, Frodo eventually arms himself with a dagger and an Elven short sword that glows in the presence of orcs.

Wearing the Blue Hat (process) allows Frodo to be a representative of process control and planning. It's the hat worn by people in management roles. If it's on his head, it is now his job to manage the thinking of other hat wearers. He wants to ensure that the thinking stays focused and moves efficiently towards a workable outcome.

Adorned with this hat, Frodo navigates a create path by becoming the person who makes sure the other hats are being used correctly. For example, when contingency plans are needed, he can direct the black hat to take action.

With his blue hat in place, Frodo asks himself, "What is the problem, and how do we define it? What is the mutual goal and desired outcome? What is the best method for moving forward?"

Knowing the mutual goal of destroying the ring, Frodo leads the hobbits to secretly follow him on a journey to a town called Rivendell. The best method to get there was to cut through an old forest while raising as little suspicion as possible.

Wearing the Yellow Hat (benefits) helps Frodo to think positively. It is the optimistic viewpoint that helps him see all the benefits of the decision and the value in it. Yellow hat thinking helps him keep going when everything looks gloomy and difficult.

In use, Frodo navigates a creative path by becoming a person unhampered by limitations or boundaries, the believer of "when there is a will, there's a way." As a yellow hat fashion icon, Frodo asks himself: "What is the best way to approach the problem? What can we do to make this work? What are the long-term benefits of this action?"

Needless to say, the long-term benefit of destroying the ring is that everyone Frodo loves remains alive. Saving his people is obviously something Frodo is willing to do. The best approach is to resist the temptation of the ring and to rely on his friends to help him.

Wearing the Green Hat (creativity) means Frodo is now dripping in creativity! This is when he has an opportunity to develop creative solutions to a problem. It is freewheeling thinking in which he gets to think with little criticism of ideas. He can also take this time to explore a range of creativity tools and resources that can help him.

While rocking this hat, Frodo navigates a creative path by asking himself: "Do alternative possibilities exist, and can we do this another way? How can we look at this problem from other perspectives? How do we think outside the box?"

Eventually, Frodo used his outside of the box thinking to successfully fool the enemies they encountered. If only he could have figured out how to ride a dragon. Maybe then his quest would have taken less time.

Whether you are on a fictional journey or in the workplace, know this - creative humans wear multiple hats because they understand that successful people navigate a creative pathway since they view things from various perspectives. This helps their creativity flourish. They also are agile about creating and responding to change in uncertain environments.

Challenges are Not Roadblocks if You're Agile

A very practical way to take your mind for a spin in the workplace is to recognize that successful people, just like everyone else, have to perceive difficulties and operate effectively regardless of circumstances. While it seems easy to celebrate new ideas, remember that viable ideas introduce changes into a system. And where there are changes, there will likely be obstacles. Creative people practice agility to navigate these challenges.

At the heart of any creative person is an agile person with an unstoppable need to learn quickly. Agile thinking is about taking everything as lessons, adjusting actions accordingly, and proceeding towards your desired outcomes. This leads to continuous improvement.

An agile person identifies challenges and doesn't let them get in the way of their success. They can figure out how to not only overcome obstacles but to turn them into opportunities. As a result, their actions prevent them from panicking when unexpected events arise.

You will inevitably hear the word *agile* used in most modern workplaces. An agile way of working is the preferred navigation model for businesses that have good customer and employee experiences at their core.

It is a creative way of breaking down and prioritizing work activities that enable a business to move quickly and readily adapt to continuous change. It originates from software development but is now often applied to all parts of a business to remain competitive in a complex and ever-changing world.

The exact origins of being an *agile thinker* are a bit mysterious. What we do know is that sometime in the 1990s a group of software industry leaders began investigating and promoting creative approaches to how software was being developed. Their focus was on a faster method to react and adapt to changing demands for technologies.

Business leaders were looking for new, highly responsive, and flexible software development practices to remain competitive in an evolving market due to the rise of online "always open" business practices. Thus began the agile management revolution that included improving speed for customer-focused solutions.

As software engineer and author Jim Highsmith puts it, "Agility is the ability to adapt and respond to change... agile organizations view change as an opportunity, not a threat."[lxxxiii] This creative thinking has transformed how many businesses work today.

Agile thinkers navigate a creative pathway to success by focusing on the development of working solutions that satisfy the needs of the customers, early and often. Importantly, these solutions don't have to be fully complete or perfect because the idea is to get them to the customers as soon as possible.

An agile thinker's goal should be to get customers to fall in love with your product and then keep delivering features to them over time. This should make sense to you if you have ever downloaded an app and had to update to "fix the bugs." The concept is aimed at focusing on constant delivery of value, gathering feedback on what is working or what isn't, and continuous improvement of the product.

The same concepts of agility can be used in everyday life. Being an agile thinker can help you deal with the many changes and challenges you will face on a regular basis.

Being able to adapt quickly is at the core of surviving the shit storm of the unknown and succeeding because you have learned from the experience. Creative people who adapt can focus on a continuous trajectory of improvement and respond to the unforeseen problems with flexibility.

The argument for being agile is that this approach helps businesses, teams, and people navigate the rapid progression of the digital revolution as it continues to transform industries, economics, and societies. **There are three main reasons or trends that should convince you of the need for agility skills.**

The first is **the workplace is a quickly evolving environment.** Customers can be demanding with their needs and investors expect growth. Business leaders act accordingly to accommodate all the fast-changing priorities and ideas thrown their way.

The second reason is **the workplace constantly introduces disruptive technology.** Established businesses and industries are being influenced by digital advancements, innovative use of new models, and automation. Examples include artificial intelligence, robotics, and the ever-expanding features of the internet. In a matter of months, you could be leading a team with job positions that do not exist today.

The last reason is **the workplace disseminates ever-increasing amounts of information.** The increased volume, availability, and distribution of information will hit you like a tidal wave. To combat this, companies need to engage in multidirectional communication channels with customers, clients, and colleagues. These channels may include things like email, chat, applications, and social media platforms. You will need your agility skills to learn this new information and master using these channels.

Before technology, traditional approaches to work were based on what is called the waterfall approach. This approach is a detailed up front planning process with large blocks of work that need to be completed before moving on to the next phase.

Today, this may be fine for simple projects in stable environments, but for anything else, this approach can be high risk. This is the reason creative people need agility.

If something changes, entire projects can grind to a stand-still and plans go out the window. Agile planning is a smarter way of working in changing environments because it allows teams to plan, complete work in shorter phases, and quickly adapt to new conditions or information.

For example, Spotify suggests that agile people, "Fail fast. Learn fast. Improve fast." At the 2016 global conference Spark the Change London, Spotify's director of engineering Marcus Frödin expressed the company's desire to be good at getting it wrong quickly and the need to be optimized for experimentation. He then presented a concept to learn from mistakes and proceeded to give examples of failures at Spotify and how they learned from them.[lxxxiv]

There are entire courses, platforms, and conferences dedicated to learning about how to navigate the agile methodology. We could go into a lot of detail on creative companies and the principles they used to demonstrate their agile management. To save time, we will share that, in general, **there are eight creative principles for adopting an agile mindset.**

Principle #1: Adapt to change. You need to be comfortable with change, and with an agile mindset, you should be constantly looking for ways to embrace it. Once way to embrace change is remember change is inevitable and normal.

What's not normal is accepting that when things change in business, you should just stick your head down and carry on your regular routines. The world around you is changing, and you need to change with it.

Principle #2: Overcome obstacles. Most people want life to be easy, like eating a scoop of gelato the size of your head as you bask in the sunshine, kind of easy. But because of obstacles, life isn't always so sweet.

Obstacles are the blockages of productivity, and you will need to use agile skills to overcome these challenges. Develop and practice these skills by remaining positive and being ready to find, by using your creative problem-solving ways, an effective solution.

Principle #3: Learn to make continuous improvements. Learning isn't something you can do once and then forget about it. It is essential that your skills and experiences in everyday life evolve. Develop and practice these skills by learning from your previous experiences and adjusting your future actions accordingly.

In all environments, you have to be agile since technology and processes are always changing. Continuous improvement is a way to stay relevant in a constantly changing world.

Principle #4: Achieve an advantage by moving faster and changing quickly. In the workplace, an agile mindset enables the business to move much faster and change direction quickly as trends emerge. Practice being fast to act, and notice what happens when you do. This will encourage you to do it again and again until acting quickly is a habit. This can help a business be first to the market with products and services, providing them with a huge competitive advantage.

Not only will this agile thinking help them move forward successfully, but it will allow them to focus on their incremental improvements. Navigators do not ignore or hide from their failures. This learning can also be practiced in your daily life.

Principle #5: Adopt a positive attitude. At this point, you might be feeling that we sound a bit redundant because we keep mentioning over and over how powerful positive thinking can be to achieving your goals. (It's even part of overcoming obstacles above.) This is because you have to be both agile and positive if you want to be successful.

Having a positive attitude applies to more than dealing with problems. It allows you to keep your mind open so you can be more creative with your success strategy. You can develop and practice this skill by focusing on your self-management and milestone achievements.

Principle #6: Have a thirst for knowledge. You guessed it, being agile is about learning and adapting. In which case, you should probably try to gain as much information as possible so you can find the solutions to whatever it is you are dealing with.

Agile thinkers are prepared to quench this thirst, but they understand that everything cannot be accomplished all at once. You can make steady and measurable progress by striving to consume knowledge daily. As a result, you will gain agility skills that can help you reach the best possible outcome.

Principle #7: Demonstrate excellence. Quality is an important aspect of being agile. There is a huge difference when it comes to realistically knowing if something is suitable, rough, or just good enough versus knowing that you have completed a comprehensive final draft. You should never underestimate the value of discussions, feedback, and guidance when it comes to the evolution of an idea.

Learn to demonstrate your work ethic in stages to the point where you won't submit a final project to your team until you are satisfied with the results of your efforts. Successful people do what needs to be done with style and personal excellence.

Principle #8: Be okay with starting over. You must try new things. Sometimes these things will fail, and you must keep learning from them. Sometimes you may even have to start over. If it is a choice between having a go with the possibility of your plan not working out and not having a go at all, then you must feel comfortable to try. There are a few ways agile people start something new.

One way is that they learn from their previous experience, and given a similar situation, they don't make the same choice next time. Another way is that they look at their situation as something that did not work now but may work out in another situation. Successful people add this new technique to their toolkit, and they feel empowered to talk about how they had to start over so others can learn from it.

Curious, creative, and innovative employees who adopt agile thinking are likely to get better results, be noticed by management, advance their careers, and secure higher paying positions. This is because they help the businesses adapt, move forward, and make an impact. Practice being one of these kinds of people.

Post this in a place (remake it with fun colors, if you'd like) where you can remind yourself that you are a creative person who can navigate challenges if you practice being an agile thinker. Don't forget to share it with us.

Be an Agile Thinker

Adapt to change.

Overcome obstacles.

Learn to make continuous improvements.

Achieve an advantage by moving faster and changing quickly.

Adopt a positive mindset.

Have a thirst for knowledge.

Demonstrate excellence.

Be okay with starting over.

Embrace Forks in the Road

It can feel overwhelming when you think about how big the world is and how changing it seems unrealistic. We do not apologize for dreaming big and pushing our boundaries beyond what people think we are capable of, and neither should you. Not all people will feel comfortable in navigating the unknown, but creative, successful people embrace and expand their tolerance in search of solutions.

When you are trying to create something new, you need to be okay with the unknown. Creating by its very nature means you are coming up with something not previously seen and/or experienced. If your current thinking and beliefs could solve your problem, they would have done it already.

The thing about the unknown is that you don't know what events are coming your way. You don't know when an "aha" moment is going to happen, and you don't know how other people will respond to your ideas.

Let's take a second to acknowledge that the potential risks that come with uncertainty can be scary. But not knowing is unavoidable when you are breaking new ground and coming up with ideas no one has ever seen before. It's part of the process. We are here to tell you that it's okay. You don't need to know everything. You just have to set yourself up to have an "aha" moment, to accept uncertainty, and to respond to change when it does happen.

Before we get into the importance of navigating uncertainty and how to get comfortable with it, it helps to understand the reasons why it feels so uncomfortable to begin with. It all begins with your brain.

In his book *The other 90%: How to Unlock Your Vast Untapped Potential for Leadership and Life*, Robert Cooper describes it clearly when he says, "A powerful part of the brain, the amygdala, wants the world to run on routine, not change... the amygdala relentlessly urges us to favor the familiar and routine. It craves control and safety, which at times can be vital." He continues, "Yet the amygdala's instincts, which have evolved over thousands of years... promote a perpetual reluctance to embrace anything that involves risk, change, or growth. Your amygdala wants you to be what you have been and stay just the way you are." This basically means people are wired for survival, and your amygdala is there to make sure you stay safe.[lxxxv]

So, if you are looking to blame something for your creativity stagnating since you were young, you can point the finger at your amygdala. This enemy will try to hijack your willingness to be uncomfortable, and as a result you can't feel any excitement on discovering the edges of your capability. Before you go off to organize a protest, remember you can teach yourself to resist this amygdala hijack by developing your skills.

Navigating uncertainty is critical for future employability. Businesses are highly likely to look for candidates who can think "on their feet" and who are open to trying new things. With such a competitive market, just doing your job will not cut it, especially since jobs where the tasks are easy are being replaced by new innovations like robots and artificial intelligence.

The work that is left behind for the humans to do is the stuff that you can't automate but rather the complex things that require a curious and creative approach. So, if you want to future-proof your career, start focusing on how you can be thinking more creatively.

If you don't want to be paralyzed and stuck because you fear the unknown, you must get comfortable with uncertainty. If all this talk has got your pulse rate up a bit, take a breath, and realize it is normal to freak out a little when you don't know what is going to happen.

Practicing getting out of your comfort zone will help. There should be at least one moment each day where you feel uncomfortable because you are in the learning zone. Be aware of your amygdala and your feelings taking over and consciously choose to follow an unfamiliar path.

Fully embrace uncertainty that comes to you. Creativity is not only a skill, it is also a state of mind.

Be open to trying new things. Be open to untested ideas. Be open to having to change your plans if you need to. Be flexible. Be adaptable. Have a bit of a reckless spirit. Ooze with confidence and seize the opportunities instead of letting fear take over. You have the potential to be a creative human. Believe.

It can be difficult to be creative in the world we live in today since it's easy to see how the technological advances have completely redefined the way we communicate. While you cannot predict the uncertainty, your creative skills can help you create a more certain future.

People used to write letters, and now with the multitude of social media apps, we can talk to virtually anyone at any time. So, if the future is unknown, how do you prepare for it? To be honest, the same way you always have. By being ready and willing to learn for an unknown world.

It's not always easy to be creative because things can change rapidly. You can't predict everything and that sucks. This is normal. All you can do is build skills to respond and adapt. Employees, the public, businesses, and emerging graduates entering the employment market need to learn and plan for evolution. They have to be ready to adapt to a constant landscape of innovation and reinvention.

Mood killer here. We live in a world of uncertainty and indecision. This can overwhelm you, make you feel anxious, and unmotivated. This can increase your chances of making wrong decisions or even paralyze your decision making. And if you let it, uncertainty can jeopardize your long-term plans and developments.

How you survive and thrive will relate to how you navigate the conditions under which you function. This is especially important to figure out in the workplace. Where else could you get paid to solve problems, make decisions, manage personal risks, and make changes?

Brake for Company Structure

Bringing your creative ideas to life is amazing. And sometimes you will feel like you just have to share all the glorious ways you'd make changes if you just got the chance to spread your ideas all over the workplace. In times like these, it's important to know that successful people have to navigate a creative pathway when they are working within a company's structure.

Within organizations, there are pre-existing policies that lay out the company's standards and expectations. In general, these policies represent how every person within the company can demonstrate excellence.

Policies can be worded in various ways. They usually include how each person can support their colleagues and how everyone should be fully committed to the team's goals. Above all, corporate policies are aligned to the organization's mission and values, and they are tied to the ideals of a specific set of professional behaviors.

Policies are important. They serve as a reference point for employees to make better choices daily. While every possible dilemma a person might encounter might not be spelled out in established policies, those policies lay out some guiding principles on how employees should make decisions and act.

Having strong policies in place is essential to building a culture of compliance. And carefully calculated policies can have massive impacts on how a company functions and how the workforce interacts on behalf of the organization.

Knowing this, we wondered, how can you successfully navigate a creative pathway to success, with policies in place? By considering these **five elements before you share your creative ideas:**

#1: Vision and purpose. This is usually written during an organization's forming stage and it helps to ensure that everyone understands what the mutual goal is. This should convey an impact that will help to encourage commitment and collaboration from the members of the team.

A successful person navigates a creative pathway to success by aligning their idea with the company's vision and purpose. For argument's sake, let's say you have an idea of introducing a delicious product that is made from beef. If the company's vision and purpose is to promote a lifestyle that excludes the exploitation of animals for the purpose of food, you should know that your idea will not be received well.

#2: Planning the work to be done. This is sometimes called "Sprint planning" because it involves breaking down the work into main tasks that can be broken down further into sub-tasks to maximize the likelihood of successful completion. It's called sprint planning because, once broken down, tasks are grouped into short phases called "sprints" which create a high-level view of what needs to be completed by when.[lxxxvi]

Each task is "estimated" based on how "big" it is or by how long it's likely to take to complete. This helps the team to decide how much can be completed in each sprint and/or how many sprints are needed to complete the work. Sprints are commonly two weeks; however, they can be longer or shorter depending on what makes sense for the project.

A successful person navigates a creative pathway to success by sharing their ideas at the right time. If they are shared before the start of the upcoming sprint, the team can take some time to review what needs to be done in the next sprint and discuss it in more detail to ensure everyone knows what to do and has the resources they need.

#3: Visual management of the work. Visually representing the workflow will allow people on the team to easily monitor the progress of the plan. It also helps the team address and fix things quickly since being off track of the goal becomes transparent. It should be divided into sprints and in columns: what's not started, in progress, ready for review, and done. Here is an example of what a creative visual management chart might look like:

Backlog	Current Sprint: Sprint 1			
	Not started	In progress	For review	Done
Sprint 2 Task	Task	Task	Task	Task
Task		Task		Task
Sprint 3 Task				

A successful person navigates a creative pathway to success by considering how their idea might interfere with what is already in the company's plans. They also consider how their idea might affect the progress of the organization's goals.

#4: Checking in frequently. This practice involves frequent team catch-ups every week and sometimes daily to discuss the work being done. In the workplace, it is referred to as team stand-ups, squad gatherings, assemblies, and/or plain old meetings. Either way, they usually take about 15 minutes and, if you're lucky, involve a nice beverage.

A successful person navigates a creative pathway to success by considering how their idea might affect these meetings or if additional team meetups or longer meeting may be necessary for their idea to take form. If additional training needs to be provided, funding these efforts is also something that needs to be considered.

#5: Formal checkpoints. At the end of the sprints and at the end of projects, it's important to take a bit of time to check in on progress. This is when you share minor and major achievements. It is also an opportunity to learn and improve as the work is being done. It is often managed through "checkpoints" called retrospectives or showcases.

A successful person navigates a creative pathway to success by shining in formal checkpoint moments. When they happen, their ideas can be displayed in presentations as both participant and observer. They are now one step closer to reaching the finish line.

Destination Greatness

Creative people are agile and embrace forks in the road as they imagine the possibilities of the world. They are curious and innovative when they share their ideas because they understand they are contributing to a team and a vision greater than themselves.

They venture into the unknown, forge a creative pathway, and are not afraid to take risks. They know that disruption keeps us moving forward.

Collectively, they reach destination greatness because they step up, learn, and adapt. This is done to help solve complex problems and make an impact. As a result, they are very valuable to employers and society alike.

FINAL THOUGHTS

Being a self-aware and honest person will help you successfully progress from learning your strengths to being part of a unified team. Maximizing your potential and the potential of others will encourage others to improve themselves. Advocating for human skills and then navigating a creative approach will help the world thrive.

In your journey to explore, learn, and change the way you feel about work, we are deeply honored you chose *Success is Human*® as a guide. Our hope is that you carry what you've learned about people throughout your life and going forward, you feel equipped to collectively obtain success.

Always remember that success can be achieved if you give energy to the learning of human skills.

We believe in you.

LEARN MORE ABOUT

maxme — SUCCESS IS HUMAN

Our team of human skills development experts have created an innovative suite of tech-enabled solutions that equip people with human skills. We do this so people can realize their potential and thrive.

From gamified apps to immersive professional blended-learning programs, everything we do is about optimizing learning for our users. Collectively, we have 200+ years of human growth experience between us.

hodie

	SOLUTION
Business	Hybrid **group learning** supported by a digital-first weekly learning plan via the Hodie app
Direct	100+ hours of gamified and curated learning. Available on iphone and Android platforms.
Schools	Interactive web-based platform "skin" for school students who can't use a phone in class. Accessed on PC or tablet.
Insights	Personalised progress reporting to maximise impact and outcomes from learning.

Maxme experiences are personalized, intuitive, and above-all engaging. We love to collaborate with other organizations to co-design learning experiences tailored to their needs. Some of our offerings include:

To find out more, simply send us a message at:
hello@maxme.com.au or hello@successishuman.com

Speaking Inquires

Renata Sguario and Erica Yvonnet speak on a variety of education and career-related topics.

Certifications

Success is Human ® facilitators can become certified to conduct human skills group workshops for learners, employers, and educators. We can provide you with presentations that can be tailored to fit your needs. To learn more, visit www.maxme.com.au

Media

Please feel free to email us directly via
hello@maxme.com.au or hello@successishuman.com

QR Code, Tools, and Resources

Learn more about human skills by visiting our Insights Library to explore free research, audio, video, special features and more. Or by signing up for Percōlāre by Maxme - our human skills monthly newsletter. You can also read about some of the case studies on our website.

And certainly, you can download book resources at www.maxme.com.au.

ENDNOTES

HONESTY

[i] Header Quote: Thomas Jefferson was a Founding Father who served as the third president of the United States from 1801 to 1809.

[ii] Part of our strengths content is brought to you in partnership with Michelle McQuaid. Michelle is a best-selling author, well-being teacher and coach who specializes in helping people to thrive so they can do their best work. For more information on her work, you can visit www.michellmcquaid.com.

[iii] Over 13 million people have taken this free character strengths survey. For more information about the VIA Character Strengths Framework, visit https://www.viacharacter.org.

[iv] Peterson, C., & Seligman, M. E. P. (2004). Character strengths and virtues: A handbook and classification. New York: Oxford University Press and Washington, DC: American Psychological Association.

[v] Gallup is a global analytics and advice firm that helps leaders and organizations solve their most pressing problems. They can be found at: https://www.gallup.com/home.aspx

[vi] Kelly, Natalie. Only 1 in 4 People use their Strengths Every day. LinkedIn, May 17, 2017. Quote taken from key insights of the L'Oréal Leadership Academy.

[vii] Brené Brown is a researcher, storyteller, and courage builder. She can be found @BreneBrown, on LinkedIn, and at www.brenebrown.com.

[viii] Pennington, David. 5 Results of Working in Your Weaknesses. Penncoaching.com Blog n.d.

[ix] Csikszentmihalyi, Mihaly. Flow: The Psychology of Optimal Experience. New York: Harper & Row, 1990.

[x] Earl Nightingale (1921-1989) was an American author and radio speaker. He dealt mostly with topics such as human character development, meaningful existence, and motivation.

[xi] Wrzesniewski, A., & Dutton, J. (2001). Crafting a job: Revisioning employees as active crafters of their work. Academy of Management Review, 26, 179 –201.

[xii] According to the website: "Evernote gives you everything you need to keep life organized – great note taking, project planning, and easy ways to find what you need, when you need it." To learn more visit www.evernote.com

[xiii] Gretchen Rubin is a best-selling author about habits and happiness. She can be found on LinkedIn, @Gretchenrubin, and at www.gretchenrubin.com.

UNITY

[xiv] Header Quote: Charles Darwin was an English naturalist, geologist, and biologist who is best known for his contributions to the science of evolution and for writing the book On the Origin of Species.

[xv] Simon Sinek is an optimist and author at Simon Sinek Inc. He can be found on LinkedIn and @simonsinek See quoted video on YouTube: Help others understand their own value to themselves.

[xvi] Larson, Carl E, and Frank M. J. LaFasto. Teamwork: What Must Go Right, What Can Go Wrong. Newbury Park, Calif: SAGE Publications, 1989.

[xvii] This team explored the highest mountain in the world at 8847.7 m, Mount Everest, which lies on the border between Nepal and Tibet. Arne Naess was the leader of the first Norwegian expedition in 1985. The expedition placed 17 climbers and Sherpas on the summit over a period of 10 days, a record at the time.

[xviii] This team was led by Ronald McNair, astronaut. They were assigned to the STS-51L mission of the space shuttle Challenger in January 1985. The primary goal of the mission was to launch the second Tracking and Data Relay Satellite (TDRS-B).

[xix] The "chuck and chew" method is a highly effective comprehension-teaching strategy that helps people acquire new concepts or knowledge. Robert J Marzano refers to this method in his book The Art and Science of Teaching: A Comprehensive Framework for Effective Instruction. Alexandria, Virginia: ASCD Publications, 2007.

[xx] Code-named "Project Aristotle," a study was conducted as a tribute to the famous philosopher's belief that it's possible to have a whole that is greater than the sum of its parts. Studying 180 teams, the researchers interviewed hundreds of executives, team leads, and team members.

[xxi] Covey, Stephen R. The 7 Habits of Highly Effective People: Restoring the Character Ethic. New York: Simon and Schuster, 1989.

[xxii] Malcolm Stevenson Forbes (August 19, 1919 - February 24, 1990) was publisher of Forbes magazine, founded by his father B.C. Forbes and today run by his son, current editor-in-chief, Steve Forbes.

[xxiii] The DiSC model is based on the work of psychologist William Moulton Marston in the 1920s. It is used as a tool to assess behavioral styles and preferences.

[xxiv] Regier, Nate. Conflict without Casualties: A field guide for leading with compassionate accountability. California: Berrett-Koehler Publishers, Inc, 2017.

MAXIMIZE

[xxv] Header Quote: Dr. Michelle Mazur is a brand messaging and marketing expert for Rebellious Business Owners. She is the author of 3 Word Rebellion: Create a One-Of-a-Kind Message That Grows Your Business Into a Movement, can be found on LinkedIn, and at www.drmichellemazur.com.

[xxvi] Albert Mehrabian was born in 1939, was a professor of psychology at the University of California, Los Angeles. This quote was based on two studies and reported in the 1967 papers "Decoding of Inconsistent Communications" and "Inference of Attitudes from Nonverbal Communication in Two Channels."

[xxvii] The Little Prince (French: Le Petit Prince) is a novella by French aristocrat, writer, and aviator Antoine de Saint-Exupéry, and it makes observations about life, adults and human nature.

[xxviii] Principles of Adult Learning & Instructional Systems Design. National Highway Institute. (n.d.). Retrieved July 15, 2022, from https://www.nhi.fhwa.dot.gov/course-search?course_no=133126A.

[xxix] Shane Snow and Joe Lazauskas, The Storytelling Edge. Wiley Publishing, February 2018. More can be learned about their work on LinkedIn, @Contently and at www.snow.academy.

[xxx] Tony Robbins is a #1 New York Times best-selling author, life and business strategist, philanthropist, and entrepreneur. More can be learned about his work on LinkedIn, @TonyRobbins, and at www.tonyrobbins.com.

[xxxi] John Moschitta is an actor, singer, writer, and fundraiser. He has been the owner of Mighty Mouth Productions, Inc. since 1982 and has been credited by the Guinness Book of World Records as the fastest talker at 586 words per minute. He can be found on LinkedIn.

[xxxii] Peter F. Drucker (1909-2005) was an Austrian-born American management consultant, educator, and writer. He said this during an interview with Bill Moyers in A World of Ideas in 1989.

[xxxiii] International Journal of Social Science and Interdisciplinary Research. "An Assessment of Listening Abilities of MBA Students." Vol. 3 (6) June 2014.

[xxxiv] Mike Irving is a Transformational Performance Coach at Advanced Business Abilities in Perth, Australia. More information can be found about his work on LinkedIn and at www.advancedabilities.com.

ADVOCATE

[xxxv] Arne Næss was a Norwegian philosopher who coined the term "deep ecology" and was an important intellectual and inspirational figure of the environment movement of the late 20th century.

xxxvi Advocate as defined in Webster's dictionary.

xxxvii The Karate Kid is a 1984 American martial arts drama film written by Robert Kamen and directed by John G. Avildsen.

xxxviii Arianna Huffington is a Greek American author, syndicated columnist, and businesswoman. She is the co-founder of the Huffington Post and the CEO of Thrive Global. She can be found @ariannahuff and on LinkedIn.

xxxix

xl Hunter Doherty "Patch" Adams (1945) is an American physician, author, and comedian. He founded the Gesundheit! Institute in 1971. Each year he also organizes volunteers from around the world to travel to dress up as clowns to bring humor to orphans and patients.

xli The happy hormones: dopamine, serotonin, oxytocin, and endorphins.

xlii Epictetus: Circa 55 – 135 A.D. was born into slavery, which likely affected his general outlook on life.

xliii Robyn L. Gobin is a clinical psychologist, assistant professor, speaker, and researcher specializing in women's mental health and interpersonal trauma. Learn more at www.robyngobin.com.

xliv The book from our ancestors is fictional, we just made this up because we think it's funny. Remember that humor is one of the VIA character strengths. At our company, working hard is inevitable but laughing hard is mandatory. We won't apologize for smiling as we work and neither should you.

xlv Study conducted in 2016, The Resilience Institute was founded in 2002. Their mission is to deliver high impact, practical, evidence-based and integrated resilience training by bringing together modern preventative medicine, positive psychology, emotional intelligence, and neuroscience. Learn more: https://resiliencei.com/about/

xlvi Directions and infographic obtained from author Amy Boone. Ethos3, Using Box Breathing to Reduce Presentation Anxiety. June 21, 2019.

xlvii Best meditation apps article: Recharge and Relax, Improve Focus and More. May 25, 2021.

xlviii If you are experiencing mental health issues you can find help from family and friends, and your GP. SAMHSA is a national helpline that is confidential, free help from public health agencies. To find substance use treatment and information call 1-800-662-4357. You can also find drug and alcohol support services online or in your area.

xlix Dweck, Carol S. Mindset: The New Psychology of Success. New York: Random House, 2006. Print.

l Pinkney, Jerry, and Aesop. The Tortoise & the Hare. First edition. New York, NY; Boston: Little, Brown and Company, 2013.

li Emanuel James Rohn, professional known as Jim Rohn was an American entrepreneur who mentored Mark R Hughes (founder of Herbalife International) and Tony Robbins in the late 1970s.

[lii] In June of 1941, the quote appeared on a newspaper page dedicated to the topics of "Home, Church, Religion, Character" within a column titled "Sermonograms." The words were credited to Eleanor Roosevelt [hnfi].

[liii] Maximilian Scheuplein and Anne-Laura van Harmelen. "The importance of friendships in reducing brain responses to stress in adolescents exposed to childhood adversity: a preregistered systematic review," Current Opinion in Psychology. Volume 45, 2022.

[liv] Thomas Alva Edison (1847-1931) was an American inventor and businessman. He developed many devices in fields such as electric power generation, mass communication, sound recording, and motion pictures.

[lv] TV Mahalingam. "These Five Business Icons Got Fired before they Became Legends," The Economic Times Bureau. March 13, 2015.

[lvi] Arianna Huffington is a Greek American author, syndicated columnist, and businesswoman. She is the co-founder of the Huffington Post and the CEO of Thrive Global. @ariannahuff and on LinkedIn.

[lvii] Gbenga Adebambo. "Perfect Flaws: Albert Einstein," The Guardian. February 11, 2017.

[lviii] Marcel Paul Pagnol (1895 – 1974) was a French novelist, playwright, and filmmaker. Regarded as an auteur, in 1946, he became the first filmmaker elected to the Académie Française.

[lix] Mohandas Karamchand Gandhi (1869 -1948) was an Indian lawyer and political ethicist who employed nonviolent resistance to lead the successful campaign for India's independence from British rule. He later inspired movements for civil rights and freedom across the world.

[lx] Search for: Life Vest Inside - Kindness Boomerang - "One Day" on YouTube and watch as the camera tracks acts of kindness as it is passed from one person to the next and manages to boomerang back to the person who began it.

[lxi] Indie Bones is made up. It's fun to pretend.

[lxii] Charles Eisenstein is an American public speaker and author. His work covers a wide range of topics, including the history of human civilization, economics, spirituality, and the ecology movement. Key themes explored include anti-consumerism, interdependence, and how myth and narrative influence culture. www.CharlesEisenstein.org

[lxiii] Nir Eyal is an Israeli-born American author, lecturer and investor known for his bestselling books, Hooked: How to Build Habit-Forming Products and Indistractable: How to Control Your Attention and Choose Your Life He can be found @nireyal, on LinkedIn, and at www.NirAndFar.com.

[lxiv] Pablo Ruiz Picasso was a Spanish painter, sculptor, printmaker, ceramicist and theater designer who spent most of his adult life in France.

[lxv] Gardner, Sarah and Albee, Dave, "Study focuses on strategies for achieving goals, resolutions" (2015). Press Releases. 266.

[lxvi] Susan Weinschenk Ph.D. Psychology Today: The True Cost of Multi-Tasking. September 12, 2012.

[lxvii] George Walton Lucas Jr. is an American film director, producer, screenwriter, and entrepreneur. Lucas is best known for creating the Star Wars and Indiana Jones franchises and founding Lucasfilm, Lucas Arts, and Industrial Light & Magic.

NAVIGATE

[lxviii] Martha Beck, Ph.D., is a bestselling author, renowned coach, and creator of Wayfinder Life Coach Training.

[lxix] Carl Benz, in full Karl Friedrich Benz (1844 – 1929) (Carl also spelled Karl). According to the Encyclopedia Britannica, he was a "German mechanical engineer who designed and in 1885 built the world's first practical automobile to be powered by an internal-combustion engine."

[lxx] Land, George & Jarman Beth (1992), Breakpoint and Beyond: Mastering the Future Today. HarperCollins Publishers.

[lxxi] Seelig, Tina Lynn. InGenius: A Crash Course on Creativity. Harper One, 2012.

[lxxii] Joseph Gordon-Levitt is an American actor and filmmaker. He is also the founder of HitRecord which is an open creative platform where anybody and everybody can creatively collaborate. His work can be found on www.hitrecord.org or on twitter @HITRECORD

[lxxiii] According to biography.com, "Steven Paul Jobs was an American inventor, designer and entrepreneur who was the co-founder, chief executive and chairman of Apple Computer. Apple's revolutionary products, which include the iPod, iPhone, and iPad, are now seen as dictating the evolution of modern technology."

[lxxiv] Newton, Isaac, 1642-1727. Newton's Principia: The Mathematical Principles of Natural Philosophy. New York: Daniel Adee, 1846.

[lxxv] Kahane, Adam. Solving Tough Problems. Berrett-Koehler Publishers, 2007.

[lxxvi] Berinato, Scott. A Framework for Understanding VUCA. Harvard Business Review, September 05, 2014.

[lxxvii] Investors.thecloroxcompany.com. "Clorox Reports Fourth Quarter and Fiscal Year 2021 Results, Provides Fiscal Year 2022 Outlook." August 3, 2021.

[lxxviii] Gonzalez, Glen. Breaking Bias: Helping employees recognize and mitigate unconscious bias, Smith Communication Partners, June, 2020.

[lxxix] Senge, Peter M. The Fifth Discipline: The Art and Practice of the Learning Organization. New York: Doubleday/Currency, 1990.

[lxxx] "Rubin's vase (sometimes referred to as The Two Face, One Vase Illusion) depicts the silhouette of a vase in black and the profiles of two inward-looking faces in white. The figure-ground distinction made by the brain during visual perception determines which image is seen." Ittelson, W. H. (1969). Visual Space Perception, Springer Publishing Company, LOCCCN 60-15818.

[lxxxi] According to illisionsindex.org, "The Young Woman, Old Woman Ambiguous Figure (also known as My Wife and My Mother-in-Law) was created by an anonymous illustrator in late 19th

century Germany and reproduced on a postcard. William Ely Hill (1887-1962), a British cartoonist, produced a later, well-known version. The later, well-known version, was first published in the magazine Puck, in 1915."

[lxxxii] De, Bono Edward. Six Thinking Hats. Toronto: Key Porter Books, 1985.

[lxxxiii] Jim Highsmith is an executive consultant with Thoughtworks, Inc. He spent 30-plus years as an IT manager, product manager, project manager, consultant, and software developer. He can be found on Twitter @jimhighsmith

[lxxxiv] Marcus Frödin is currently (as of 2019) the VP of Engineering for Marketplace and the General Manager of the Core Platform at Spotify. He can be found on Twitter @marcusf

[lxxxv] Cooper, Robert. The other 90%: How to Unlock Your Vast Untapped Potential for Leadership and Life, Crown Archetype, 2002.

[lxxxvi] Severino, Simon. Strategy Sprints: 12 Ways to Accelerate Growth for an Agile Business. Kogan Page, 2022.

ABOUT THE AUTHORS

Renata Sguario is an experienced senior executive with almost three decades of specializing in business transformation at leading companies in Australia and abroad. Renata's passion to develop human potential led her to founding Maxme, a human skills development company, with a focus on providing young job seekers the much-needed arsenal to secure and thrive in their dream job.

Erica Yvonnet is a sought-after speaker and facilitator who develops compelling content that informs, generates interest, and makes a difference. Prior to being an author, Erica spent 15 years as a language arts educator and professional developer in the USA school system. She currently works and resides in the state of New Jersey.

NOTE FROM THE AUTHORS

Word-of-mouth is crucial for any authors to succeed. If you enjoyed *Success is Human*, please leave a review online—anywhere you are able. Even if it's just a sentence or two. It would make all the difference and would be very much appreciated.

Thanks!
Renata Sguario and Erica Yvonnet

We hope you enjoyed reading this title from:

www.blackrosewriting.com

Subscribe to our mailing list – *The Rosevine* – and receive **FREE** books, daily deals, and stay current with news about upcoming
releases and our hottest authors.
Scan the QR code below to sign up.

Already a subscriber? Please accept a sincere thank you for being a fan of
Black Rose Writing authors.

View other Black Rose Writing titles at
www.blackrosewriting.com/books and use promo code
PRINT to receive a **20% discount** when purchasing.

www.ingramcontent.com/pod-product-compliance
Lightning Source LLC
Chambersburg PA
CBHW071955070526
44583CB00015B/1199